Philosophy, Technique and Fulfillment

Philosophy, Technique and Fulfillment

An Explanatory Review and Presentation of His Holiness Shri Maharishi Mahesh Yogi's Transcendental Meditation

Prof. H.S. Shivaswamy

2007

Philosophy, Technique and Fulfillment

CONTENTS

INTRODUCTION

INTRODUCTION

In my first compilation of the comparative study on "Relaxation response, meditation and Yoga", I had written about Transcendental Meditation briefly explaining the technique and its practice. I had compared therein, Transcendental Meditation with Relaxation Response and the method of yoga of Patanjali.

Recently about a year back, I could get access to a copy of the book "Science of Being and art of Living—Transcendental meditation" by Sri Maharishi Mahesh Yogi. I made an in-depth study of the book and found that it is one of the rare scientific books ever produced in modern times. Maharishi has dealt in his book in a very comprehensive way the philosophy, technique and practice of Transcendental Meditation. He has based his system of Transcendental Meditation on the firm basis of the philosophy of the Upanishads and Bhagavad-Gita. He has shown therein how the regular practice of Transcendental Meditation directly leads one to the field of the transcendental consciousness which lies within oneself, as one's own inseparable Self.

His method of approach is highly scientific. He observes that the existence of the never changing, unmanifested absolute is unbounded and eternal in status, and that the absolute is beyond all the ever-changing relative existence of forms and phenomena. He further sees no contradiction between his own statement about the absolute, and the findings of Dr. Albert Einstein's theory of relativity, which concerns itself only with the relative existence of forms and phenomena.

Maharishi claims that the system of Transcendental Meditation provides a direct and simple technique which leads man directly to the experience of transcendental consciousness.

His view on the phenomenon of experience, bondage and liberation from bondage, deserve the attention of all seekers of truth and aspirants. He has examined, how this question has been misunderstood and misinterpreted for the past many centuries by the metaphysicists and on account of this mis-interpretation how the genuine seekers of truth and aspirants have been deprived of a direct path to God realization.

His view on the ideology of surrender require close attention. He distinguishes clearly the through of Being from the state of being. His statement that true surrender is always on the level of being and not on the level of thinking deserves the close examination by the devotees and seekers of truth.

He has touched on Karma, its inexorable nature and its bondage and explains how Transcendental Meditation infuses the mind with being and liberates one from bondage of karma.

He has spoken exclusively about the fulfillment of life, fulfillment of religion, psychology and philosophy brought about by the practice of Transcendental Meditation and these have been dealt with.

Speaking about fulfillment of modern psychology, he expresses his sense of apprehension and discouragement. He expresses his doubts about the roles of psychology in reminding man that his past was miserable or his surroundings and circumstances were unfavourable. Regarding fulfillment of psychology he refers to Bhagavad-Gita and its teaching, where the psychological teaching of the Gita reveals a master technique for establishing the co-ordination between the individual mind and the cosmic mind.

Maharishi also examines the different paths to God realization. These have been dealt with in detail.

In short, Maharishi has left nothing untouched which has bearing upon the development of the human personality in its physical, spiritual and mental aspects brought about by the practice of Transcendental Meditation. He says that the regular practice of Transcendental Meditation (Karma) represents 'Karma Yoga'.

I find, that in India, the philosophy and fulfillment of Transcendental Meditation, so exquisitely brought out by Maharishi in his book has not been widely read and understood. I consider that my explanatory presentation of the outstanding features of Transcendental Meditation and its philosophy brought out in this book will serve even though to a small extent, in bringing to the attention of the readers some outstanding features of Transcendental Meditation which may help them to take up to the practive of Transcendental Meditation, thereby contributing to the upliftment of the individual, society and nation. Towards that end I have dedicated my explanatory study.

I express my sincere thanks to my son Dr. H.S.Mruthyunjaya, my grandson H.M.Vivek, Mrs. Vijaya Jayatheeratha and my granddaughter Nayantara Golapakrishna for helping me in various tasks during my writing of this book.

Dated : 15.01.1993   **H.S.SHIVASWAMY**

PART—I

Basic philosophy and the art of Transcendental Meditation

Philosophy unravels the law of the perfect unity of the reality, underlying everything that exists in the universe. That unity is termed "Brahman" in the Upanishads.

> Taittiriya Upanishad speaks of Brahman thus :
> "that from which all these entities and beings are born,
> that in which being born, they live,
> that into which, in the end they enter,
> know that, that is Brahman".
> (Tai.Up. III 1)

HIS HOLINESS SHRI MAHARISHI MAHESH YOGI in his book "Science of being and Art of LIVING—Transcendental Meditation" CALLS THIS Brahmin of the Upanishads as Being.

We shall describe the philosophy underlying Transcendental Meditation. As developed by Sri Maharishi in his book— Science of being and Art of living—Transcendental Meditation.

Being define :

Maharishi defines Being as existence. Being or existence finds expression the different aspects of living; thinking, speaking, doing, experiencing, feeling. All aspects of life have their basis in Being. Existence is abstract, that which exists is concrete.

Maharishi says existence is life itself, while that which exists is the ever changing phenomenal phase of the never changing reality of existence. Existence is the abstract aspect of life. All the concrete phases of life covering all aspects of life of the individual, namely body, mind, thinking, speaking, acting, behaving, experiencing, influencing the surroundings, including all aspects of cosmic existence find their basis on the abstract aspect of life.

Being is the ultimate reality of everything that existed, that is existing, or that will exist. It is eternal, unbounded, and the basis of all the phenomenal existence of the cosmic life. It is the source of all time, past, present and future, of space and causation. It is described as the be-all and end-all of existence. It is the all pervading eternal field of the almighty creative intelligence Upanishads declare being as "I am Brahman" (Br. Up. 1-4-10): "That thou art"—(Ch. Up. 6-16-3). "this self is Brahman" (Ma.Up.-2) "Consciousness is Brahman" (It-Up-III-3). "All this is Brahman" (Ma.Up-2). It is established by experience that being is bliss consciousness.

Being is the source of all thinking, the source of all existing creation. It is found by an experiencer to be beyond relative existence, where the experiencer or mind is all left awake by itself, in full awareness of itself, without any object of experience. The conscious mind then reaches the state of pure consciousness which is the source of all thinking. The almighty creative intelligence of the absolute, is the source of all intelligence. Being is the source of all power. It is the source of all nature, and of the natural laws, which sustain the different forms and phenomena of relative creation.

The essential nature of being is absolute bliss consciousness. It is Sat which never changes, Chit which is consciousness. Ananda which is bliss. Being is the fundamental of life. Without being aware of the fundamental of life which is absolute bliss consciousness, Maharishi says, that life is like a building without a foundation. The life of the individual without the realization of being, which is absolute bliss consciousness, is baseless, meaningless and fruitless.

Being as the basis of life gives it meaning and makes it fruitful. Being is the living presence of God in man. It is the reality of life. It is eternal truth. It is the absolute in eternal freedom. Man should strive for its realization.

Being as the essential constituent of creation

Physical science tells us that the whole of creation is built up of layers of energy, one inside the other. The subtlest is at the inner most stratum of creation and builds up around itself, into different qualities becoming bigger and bigger.

Underneath the subtlest layers of all that exists in the relative field of creation, is the abstract, absolute field of pure being, which is unmanifested and transcendental. It is neither matter nor energy. It is pure being, the state of existence-absolute-bliss consciousness.

The state of pure existence underlies all that exists. Everything is the expression of this pure existence, absolute being, which is the essential constituent of all relative life.

The one eternal, unmanifested absolute being, manifests itself in many forms of lives and existences in creation. With the increase in our knowledge f the finer strata of existence, we gain advantage of that knowledge, and grow in our understanding of life. Our life becomes more powerful, more creative and more useful. Our aspirations also are found increasing. The knowledge of Being as the basis of all creation and as the ultimate essential constituent of everything that exists in the universe, raises the stature of all aspects of life to the unbounded status of the absolute existence. Relative life raises its stature to the absolute standard of existence, and based on this, stability and permanence are imparted to the relative field.

As a result of the unraveling of the knowledge of Being, energy, intelligence and creativity rise to their limitless values. Individual life overcomes its limitations, and gains the status of unbounded eternal cosmic existence. Individual life thereby gets its identity, stability and permanence. Maharishi says, that this is the glorious aspect of the discovery that being is the essential constituent of creation.

Being the Omnipresent :

Maharishi explains the Omnipresence of Being thus. As the essential constituent of creation it is present in every stratum of creation. It is present in all forms words, smells, tastes, and objects of tough. It is present in all the senses of perception and organs of action. It is present in every phenomena. It is present both in the doer and the work done. It is pervasive in all directions—north, south, east, west. It is in all times, past, present and future. It is present in front of man, behind him, to the left and right of him, above him, below him, in him, everywhere and under all circumstances, as the essential constituent of creation. It permeates everything. It is the omnipresent God for those who know and understand it, feel it and live it in their lives.

The entire creation in different forms and phenomena is the field of consciousness. Consciousness is the radiation from the center of pure Being. From the inexhaustible source of being, bliss consciousness radiates, and as it proceeds further from its source, the degree of bliss diminishes. We could speak of consciousness appearing in all subtle and gross forms of life.

It is seen that people whose hearts and minds are not sufficiently cultured and whose vision concentrates on the gross, will concern themselves with the surface value of life only. They only see quality of matter and energy. They function only on the surface of life and things. They do not dives deeper and find the pure ever present omnipresent being, in all its purity and abundance of splendour, joy and happiness, and in its never changing status. On the other hand they concern themselves only with the ever changing phase of forms and phenomena, of matter and energy, and off mind and individual.

Pure Being is of transcendental nature, because of its status as the essential constituent of creation. It is finer than the finest in creation. Because of its transcendental nature, it is precluded from the purview of the senses, which are primarily formed to give only experience of the manifested reality of life. It is also not exposed to the perception by the mind, because, the mind is connected for the most part with the senses, and for any experience, the mind has to associate itself with the senses and come in contact with the manifested world of forms and phenomena.

Experience shows that being is the essential basic nature of the mind, but since it commonly remains tuned with the senses, which project outwards toward the manifested realms of creation, the mind misses or fails to appreciate its own essential nature, just like the eyes, which are unable to see themselves. Everything can be seen through the eyes except themselves. Similarly when the mind is engaged in the projected field of manifested diversity, it fails to appreciate its own essential nature namely Being. Being is at the root of everything. It supports the existence of life and creation, but yet remains abstract and not exposing itself. It's pure almighty omnipresent nature finds. It's dignified presence in man, as the basis of ego, intellect, mind, senses, body and surroundings. But it is not easily seen, recognized or understood. Yet it underlies all creation and is its essential constituent.

Maharishi compares Being to a powerful business magnate who is rarely found in the corridors of the actual place of business, who remains obscure and yet effectively controls his business operations. In order to see him, it is necessary to meet him in seclusion far from the main activity of the business scene. Maharishi says, likewise, the all controller of the universe being present everywhere, influencing everything and remaining at the basis of the conduct of all universal activity and phenomenal life, himself, dwells in the silent chamber of the heart of everyone and everything.

Being, the field of eternal life :

Absolute being and its relationship with the relative universe can be understood by an example. Absolute being can be compared to a limitless ocean of life, silent and eternally existing. The different aspects of the phenomenal creation can be compared to the ripples and waves of the vast limitless oceans of eternal Being. All the forms and phenomena of the relative existence and the ever changing states of life in the world, have their basis in the eternal life of the omnipresent being.

Being is the unlimited vastness of pure existence, or pure consciousness, the essential constituent and content of life. It is the field of unlimited, unbounded eternal life, pure intelligence, pure existence, the absolute.

Having thus found that Being is the field of eternal life, on the practical level of an individual's life what is encouraging is the fact, that the ever changing phenomenal phase of daily life in the world can be supplemented with the unlimited power of eternal life of Being. How this is achieved in the different phases of individual life will be dealt later.

Being the basis of all living :

Being is the essential constituent of all creation. It is the source of all activity in the individual. All human activity comprising the complex and diversified field of day to day life, is founded and sustained by it. The unmanifested and transcendental being manifests itself in the form of 'prana' and mind, which is the level of thinking and breathing. Our life starts with breathing and thinking. Therefore we see that all activity in our life is based on the absolute eternal field of Being.

The start of activity is from the level of thinking. The start of thinking is at the level of the transcendental Being. Therefore, we find Being is at the basis of all activity, behaviour and the variety of ways and forms of living.

Being is therefore the basis of all living just as the sap and root, is the basis of the tree. If we can take care of the sap, the whole tree would be taken care of.

If we can take care of Being the whole field thinking and doing will be taken care of. Maharishi says "The whole field of life can be glorified by consciously taking care of Being". (Page 28 Science of being and art of living—T.M. By Shri Maharishi Mahesh Yogi).

Being the plane of cosmic law :

Cosmic means all inclusive. It means of the entire universe. By cosmic law we mean the rule of procedure that governs the purpose of cosmic existence and evolution. It means the rule of mode of action of cosmic creative intelligence, which creates, maintains, and dissolves the universe.

In the universe, we find life is progressing. Something is created. It develops to its fullest extent and in the end begins to decay. It decays, and becomes transformed again.

We find that things are changing in the universe. Besides changes we see that there is maintenance. Life maintains itself, and evolves at the same time. The aspect of maintenance constitutes stability; the aspect of evolution is one of change.

Under cosmic law we have to consider these two factors; one is the factor of stability and the other is the factor of change in the universe. The two factors are found simultaneously.

In the universe, something is created, maintained, and while it is maintained, it evolves and reaches the height of evolution and dissolution continues on, and in its continuity, the life of the universe goes on. When we are speaking cosmic or universal law, all the different features of the universe, involving creation of things, creation of life, maintenance of the created things of life, evolution of the maintained life, and ultimately dissolution, all these have to be considered. Maharishi, to explain what cosmic law is, gives an example. He takes Hydrogen and Oxygen, which are both gases.

They combine to form water (H2O). Here the qualities of gas have changed to the qualities of water. But 'H' and 'O' remain 'H' and 'O'. Again the water freezes and is transformed into the qualities of ice. But essential constituents 'H' and 'O' remain the same. Hydrogen and Oxygen remaining the same means, that there is some force, some law or system, which maintains the integrity of Hydrogen and Oxygen, but yet, there are certain laws which keep on changing the qualities of gas to water, and water into ice.

From the above, it is clear that there is one law which does not allow the integrity of Hydrogen and Oxygen to change, and further, that law itself does not change. The law which does not allow Hydrogen and Oxygen to change into anything else, is itself unchanging, uniform and eternal. Allowing Hydrogen and Oxygen to go through all the different levels of creation, the law which is itself unchanging, maintains the integrity of Hydrogen and Oxygen.

We see in the universe different levels of creation, in different forms which keep on evolving. We see the appearance of new qualities. These new qualities which appear are necessarily due to new laws which come into play. All these new laws come into play, even while that eternal law remains in its unchanging state. All the changes in the manifold creation in the universe take place on the unchanging platform of the essential constituent of creation which is absolute and eternal. This gives an idea of what the cosmic law is.

The law that never changes, ever maintains the integrity of the ultimate essential constituent of creation. Therefore, this cosmic law is such, that it never changes and remains eternal. While it never changes, it brings forth newer and newer laws at different states of creation. This results in the different states of creation, the different forms and phenomena.

The absolute state of pure consciousness is of unmanifested nature, and ever remains as that, by virtue of the never changing cosmic law.

This cosmic law is the basis of all the laws of nature and all the laws of evolution.

Being the Absolute and the Relative :

Maharishi gives the analogy of an ocean to explain the absolute and the relative states of existence. Just as the ocean ranges from the never changing eternal silence at its bottom to the great activity of an ever changing nature on the surface of the waves, so also, the unbounded field of Being ranges from the unmanifested, absolute eternal state, to the gross, relative and ever changing states of phenomenal life.

The eternal silent state of the ocean at the bottom, corresponds to the never changing, eternal, absolute state of existence. The ever active phase of the ocean at the surface represents the relative phase of Being and corresponds to the world of forms and phenomena in which we live.

Both these states, the absolute and the relative, are the states of Being. Being is thus eternally never changing in its absolute state, and it is eternally ever changing in its relative states.

This reveals that being or the unmanifested absolute has two sides to its essential nature; one is absolute and the other relatives. The entire field of life from the individual to the cosmos, is nothing but an expression of the eternal absolute, never changing Omnipresent being, in its relative ever changing phase of existence.

As we have seen before, Hydrogen and Oxygen atoms in one state exhibit the properties of gas, in another they combine and exhibit the qualities of water, yet, in another state, they combine and exhibit the qualities of solid ice. But in all these states, the essential constituent, 'H' and 'O' remains the same.

Just like Hydrogen and Oxygen, remaining in their never changing state as Hydrogen and Oxygen are found exhibiting different forms and qualities, in a like manner, Being, remaining in it's never changing eternal absolute character, is found expressing itself in the forms and phenomena of the diverse creation.

Maharishi points out that the above statement of his, might look to some of the scientifically minded people as being contradictory to the established theories of physical science. Maharishi refers in this connection, in particular to Dr. Albert Einstein's theory of relativity which places everything in the universe, as being relative, and which accounts only in terms of relativity the existence of the different world's forms and phenomena. But Maharishi points out that he see no contraction between his own statement regarding Being, and the theory of relativity propounded by dr. Albert Einstein. Einstein was not wrong, says Maharishi, because his theory of relativity concerned itself only with the manifested field of creation which belongs to the realm of physical science. According to Maharishi Einstein in his attempt to establish the unified field theory, seems to have been clearly aware of the possibility of one ultimate basis of all diversity, one common basis of all relative creation. If, and when, physical science arrives at what Einstein was trying to foresee in his attempts to establish the unified field theory, one element will have been established as the source of all relative creation. The day may not be far off, says maharishi, when theoretical physics will establish the principle of unity in the midst of diversity, as the basic unity of material existence.

Such a discovery, maharishi says, of this one field of basic unit underlying all material existence will then mark the ultimate achievement in the history of development of physical science. The quest of the human mind, will naturally then, turn from the world of physical science, to the science of mental phenomena. Theories of mind, intellect, and ego, will then supersede the bindings of physical science As the investigative scientific mind pursues its onward search, into the nature of the reality in the field of the mind, then, as a crowning achievement, will be found located the field of pure consciousness or the field of the transcendental, lying beyond all relative existence of material and mental phenomena. The ultimate field of the transcendental Being, lying beyond the field of mental phenomena, will thus be found to be the truth of life in all its phases, relative and absolute. Thus it will be found that the science of Being transcends the science of mind, which in turn transcends the science of matter, and the science of matter in turn transcends the diversity of material existence.

For the benefit of the readers, we can sum up the above conclusions arrived at by shri Maharishi in the course of his thesis.

1. Being is the ultimate reality of all that exists.
    It is unmanifested, absolute and transcendental.
2. Everything in the universe is of a relative order.
3. The truth is that eternal Being, ultimate life principle of unmanifested nature is expressing itself in different forms and phenomena in the relative existence, maintaining the status quo of all that exists.
4. The absolute and relative existence are the two aspects of one and the same reality namely, eternal Being.
5. Eternal Being is thus both absolute and relative.

Being, as the Eternal and Ultimate Reality

Maharishi explains how one can directly experience Being. The mind is first made to experience the subtle state of a sound or through, and is then led on in a systematic manner, to the sublet limit of experience. The mind then transcends, this subtlest limit reality, the field of transcendental bliss consciousness.

Bhagavd Gita speaks of this eternal Self within us thus, "He is uncleavable; he cannot be burnt; he can be neither wetted nor dried. He is eternal, all pervading, unchanging and immovable. He is the same for ever;" (Bhagavd Gita II—24).

"He is said to be unmanifest, unthinkable, and unchanging. Knowing him as such, thou shouldst not grieve". (B.G. II—25).

The Upanishads speak of Being as the ultimate reality, the Brahman, the supreme ultimate absolute, eternal and imperishable. Both the hymns of the Vedas and the Bhagavad Gita speak of the glory of this imperishable self, being, the supreme ultimate reality. The Panishads speak of the glory of Being, the Brahman, the ultimate reality as, Sat-Chit-Ananda and find it within man, as his own inseparable self. They reveal the ultimate truth in the expressions, "That Thou Art", "I am Brahman", "This Atman is Brahman", "All this is Brahman", "Consciousness is Brahman". These expressions, Maharishi says, have been the solace and source of inspiration to millions of people from times immemorial. The Indian philosophy expounds the oneness of life, as the ultimate reality, the absolute Being.

The idea of Being, as the ultimate reality is contained in the oldest records of Indian thought. The eternal Vedas crowned with the philosophy of the Uapnishads, bring out the relative and the absolute, as the two aspects of one and the same reality, Brahman, the absolute Being, which though unmanifest in its absolute existence, appears manifest as the relative diversity of creation.

Life is nothing but Being in all its phases of absolute and relative existence. Oneness of Being permeates the diversity of life, and the imperishable Being permeates the ever changing perishable universe.

Maharishi in particular points out that the study of Being on account of its abstract nature has until recently been considered to be mystical in nature, and has been kept out of the purview of the common man. The common man has therefore been deprived fro hundreds of generations past, the glory of the enlightenment and experience of Being.

Now, with the availability of a systematic way of experiencing the ultimate transcendental Being, the transcendental reality not only steps out of the mystical field, into the daylight of modern scientific enquiry, but becomes the solace and refuge of man. Man gets the strength, vitality and identity in his own self, against all the forces of discord, disharmony and fears of annihilation thrown by man's increasing knowledge and power in various sciences. Further, the knowledge of Being as the eternal and ultimate reality within one's own self, provides man, encouragement and a means to supplement and reinforce his own ever changing phase of individual life, on the profound basis of the never changing status of being, the eternal and ultimate reality. Man thereby finds his identity and stability enshrined in his own eternal self within.

Prana and being :

Being, as we have seen is the absolute existence of the unmanifested reality. It's tendency to vibrate and manifest is referred to as prana. Being vibrates by virtue of prana and manifests. Prana is thus the expression of unmanifested Being. When Being assumes a subjective nature, being becomes mind. Assuming an objective nature it becomes matter. Remaining innocent or pure it serves as a link, between the subject and object, establishing the subject-object relationship and making possible the start of the multiple creation in the relative field.

In this way the very nature of Being starts the process of creation, and evolution begins.

Prana is thus seen to be the power of being, the vital force of life and creation, which is latent in unmanifested Being, and comes into play in the process of manifestation of the relative field of subjective and objective creation. In actual creation it is seen as the medium through which matter and mind are linked to consciousness. Without this vital medium, consciousness cannot express itself in the external world through the mind.

Mind and Being :

Maharishi describes mind as a wave in the ocean of unmanifested absolute Being. Unmanifested absolute Being, stimulated by its own nature appears as mind, just as an ocean stimulated by the wind appears as a wave.

Karma acts as the force of wind to produce a wave of the mind in the ocean of unmanifested Being.

It may therefore be said that prana, supplemented by the influence of Karma becomes the mind.

Mind's identity in the present life is determined by the Karma of the past life. The level of evolution which the mind had gained in the past life, determines its status in the present life, and based on the karma of the past life, the mind starts its journey in the present life. Karma is inert (Jada), the inert Karma supplemented by the life force, prana, gives rise to the mind. This mind is therefore a composite of prana and karma, and through prana, it is connected with unmanifested being. Mind is thus the second stage in the process of manifestation or creation, the first being prana. This clarifies the position of the mind in the field of creation and its relationship with Being, the ultimate absolute.

Next, Maharishi deals with the original of individual mind from Prana and Karma. Prana is the first expression of cosmic intelligence. When Prana is reflected upon by Karma, the prana gains individuality and appears as individual mind. This the individual mind is found to be the reflection of cosmic mind or cosmic intelligence on Karma. Just as prana is the manifesting expression of the eternal ocean of unmanifested Being, individual mind is the reflection of cosmic intelligence on karma. It is thus seen that before the creation of the mind, there existed in principle the agency of karma. This leads us to conclude that there was creation before creation. The cycle of creation and dissolution is the eternal cycle in the eternity of Being. In the process of creation there comes mind to be, because there existed a mind before, which created some karma which Maharishi conceives therefore, of two realities at the basis of creation. One is the eternal reality of absolute Being and the other is the reality of karma. The reality of karma is also eternal in the sense, that, although it lies in the ever-changing field of relative existence, it continues to be eternally present in the ever continuing cycle of action, experience and impression, and thereby attains its eternal status. Maharishi next deals with the subject of the subtle mechanics of creation. The impression of an experience, is said to be the finest remains of the karma or action. It maintains its existence at the finest level of the mind, almost at the meeting point of the mind and prana. It is just at that plane that the creation begins, where Being becomes mind, and by virtue of the finest impression of karma, prana simultaneously assumes the role of the mind. Then the next step in creation, is almost the simultaneous production in principle, of the mechanism of the senses of perception to enable the mind to function and to materialize the reality of mind and senses. Then matter comes into being, to provide the physical machinery through which the five senses of perception could find their expression, thus justifying the validity of their creation. These senses of perception and the physical machinery exist and act as the agents of the mind to carry forward the process of evolution and creation.

This is the process of the formation of the senses nervous system and body.

Being, as we have seen previously, is the unbounded eternal ocean of absolute life. It is of transcendental nature and hence is without any attribute. It is experienced, but the experience is in its own field of transcendental existence of pure consciousness, where the experiencing mind transcends all the fields of relative experience and becomes one with Being, and attains the state of Being. It is no longer then, the conscious mind. Maharishi adds that this state of attribute less absolute existence lies completely beyond imagination. It cannot be intellectually conceived, or understood or expressed.

In creation, it is not being that manifests. Being is transcendental and attribute-less. It is therefore, not in a position to manifest or to resist manifesting. It cannot therefore create. Speaking about creation, Maharishi observes thus: It is the reflection of Being on Karma, or, the reflection of Karma on being that becomes the tendency to create, thereby gaining the attributes of prana. From that point, based on that reflection, the whole creation starts, leaving Being to remain unchanged in its eternal status of the absolute. Thus nothing happens to absolute Being and creation begins in its multifarious forms and phenomena based on the instrumentality of karma, propelled by prana, and carried out by the mind, leaving Being untouched.

It is also clear that because Being is omni-present all the multiplicity of creation is pervaded by it. Nothing is without it. Everything is it. But creation does not involve Being. Being does not participate in it, and at the same time, Being pervades the whole creation. Similarly mind does not involve Being. It is irrespective of Being and at the same time its essential nature is Being.

It is the wheel of karma that keeps on creating, evolving and dissolving the phenomenal creation, in cycles of existence and nonexistence of the cosmos as a whole and the individual finds his share in it as a part of it.

Maharishi clarifies further. In essence life is eternal and absolute. In reality, nothing but that alone exists. The ever changing relative forms and phenomena, and the entire cosmic existence find their life in eternal Being, but their phenomenal phase of existence is based on the plane of karma. But karma has no absolute status in itself. The relative phase of creation finds an ever lasting status in the cycles of creation and dissolution. Thus there are two foundations of life. One is the absolute being and the other is karma.

We have seen previously that Being, in its essential nature is the absolute existence. Hence it alone can be accepted as the ultimate reality of life and existence. Being is absolute, and being so, is attribute-less and cannot create.

It is thus found that absolute attribute less eternal Being is the ultimate reality of existence and by virtue of its own nature, the process of creation, evolution, and dissolution continues eternally without affecting in any way the absolute status of eternal being.

Karma and Being :

Maharishi defines karma as action or activity. We have seen previously that karma is opposed to the essential nature of Being. Being is just to be. Being is absolute existence, while karma is the instrument through which the cycle of creation, evolution and dissolution is kept going continuously.

No karma can ever reach the state of Being. The state of Being is for ever there, the same omnipresent, transcendental, absolute existence, eternally. But moving in the wheel of karma, the life of the individual always remains in the field of relative existence. The life of the individual and that of the cosmos, is being created, maintained and dissolved by the force of karma. Every individual and all the beings in the world are subject to the force of karma. The force of karma keeps on maintaining the life of the individual in the relative field and the individual goes on from birth to birth, and is constantly kept out of the realm of pure being. IN maharishi's words, the individual misses the glory of being. Any process of brining karma to an end, would certainly result in the individual attaining the state of Being.

If therefore a way could be found to avoid the grip of karma, that would be the way to attain the state of eternal Being. Maharishi suggests that, by adopting a technique of minimizing the activity of experiencing, the mind could be led on, in a systematic manner to the subtlest field of activity, and then transcending the subtlest state, the mind could arrive at the state of Being, the field of eternal life.

He points out that this fact f the nature of Being and karma being essentially opposed to each other, has been greatly misinterpreted by many, who did not know the technique of minimizing the force of karma and coming out of its influence. Such people of incomplete vision, says Maharishi, who read in metaphysical books that absolute bliss consciousness is opposed to the nature of karma, evolve their own theories. They argue that the life activity of man in the world opposes the state of absolute bliss consciousness. This misunderstanding has been responsible for creating a gulf between spiritual and material values of life, and such an outlook on life has existed for many centuries past. Such an attitude has led to a general belief among the people that man's life activity in the world is incompatible with the state of absolute bliss consciousness, and to gain the state of bliss consciousness, one has therefore to cease involving himself in the active worldly life. This has let to the belief that attainment of spiritual salvation is only possible for those who withdraw from the active life of the society, and take to a life of renunciation and lead an ascetic life. Such an attitude has been spiritually degrading to the life of the common people and householders, and has done immense harm and has set the clock back in the spiritual development of the common people.

Maharishi argues that it is true that the nature of the absolute and the relative, the nature of Being and karma, are opposed to each other and are incompatible. This should not in itself deter a householder from attaining the state of eternal life which exists within himself, even while being engaged fully in the activities of the world. Maharishi at this stage puts before the world his unique technique of Transcendental Meditation, by the practice of which, it would be possible for mankind, in Maharishi's words, "to glorify the field of karma by the light of Being". (Science of Being and Art of Living—T.M. Page 42). He further observes, "This is the point that hundreds of generations within the past many centuries have missed". Science of Being and Art of Living—T.M. Page 42). The knowledge that it only needs skill in action, to accomplish this glorification of karma has been missed by man-kind. He mentions this, as the main reasons for the growing suffering, misery, and tension and the prevailing attitude of negativity in all fields of man's life. He emphasizes that this mistake must be corrected for the good of the people. It should be realized by all that through the system of Transcendental Meditation, it should be possible for every mind to come out of the relative state of experience, and attain the transcendental state, the mind becomes infused with the full value of being, because in the field of the transcendent, it is out of the relative field of karma. It ceases to be individual mind, and becomes one with absolute eternal being. When the mind has thus gained this state of eternal being, the force of karma draws the mind back again to the relative field of activity. When the mind comes back into the relative field of activity, it realizes by its own experience, that the state of transcendental being was certainly more alluring, and better in its unlimited status of absolute bliss, than the relative state of transitory joy and happiness in the field of activity.

Further, the state of bliss consciousness of the transcendent makes a real impact upon the nature of the mind. It is found that the mind becomes more powerful having had experience of the unbounded state of limitless bliss consciousness. When the mind comes out into the relative field of karma, where time, space and causation, keep everything within limited boundaries, the mind retains some of the unbounded status in its nature. With repeated and regular practice of Transcendental Meditation, the mind becomes familiar with the transcendental state of consciousness and when it comes out into the field of relative experience, its nature is transformed to a much higher state of consciousness.

Speaking about the results accruing from the practice of Transcendental Meditation, Maharishi observes "the practice of Transcendental Meditation results in such a great impact of the nature of Being on the nature of the mind, that the mind begins to live the nature of eternal Being and yet continues to behave and experience in the field of relative existence. This is the tremendous value to the mind achieved through the association of transcendental Being in the day-to-day practical life in the world" (Page 43 — Science of Being and Art of Living—T.M).

He refer to the technique of Transcendental Meditation. Whereby the field of karma is glorified by the light of Being, as the skill in action which harmonises the value of Being with the value of the field of activity or karma. He explains that this skill lies in brining the action of the mind to recede to its source and to start the conscious activity from the source of thought. This is the skill in action which succeeds in infusing the power of Being into the field of karma, through the instrumentality of the mind.

He says that this skill in action glorifies the mind at all levels and at the same time leaves the mind free from the bondage of karma, because the mind is then established in eternal bliss consciousness. He gives the example of a candle light losing its relative significance in the bright sunlight. In a similar manner, in the eternal light of the absolute bliss, the relative joys of life lose their attraction. This is said to be the loss of the binding influence of karma, under the influence of the experience of the absolute bliss of eternal being.

The skill in action in first bringing the activity to nil and from there starting to act, is compared by Maharishi, to an arrow pulled back on the bow as far as possible until it reaches the state of no activity, and then shooting it by just releasing the catch without any effort. So the skill ion action is just like pulling the arrow back and then releasing it. It will shoot ahead with the least amount of effort, with the maximum force. So, likewise, the skill in action consists in bringing the activity of the mind to a state of stillness, and from that point starting the conscious activity. The energy necessary to perform the action will be least. The action performed brings the greatest results and the doer will cultivate a state of eternal freedom. The doer will be acting, being established in eternal Being, and therefore will not be under the binding influence of action or karma. This is said to be the true skill in action. It is therefore, clear as

Maharishi points out, that even though the nature of karma and the nature of being are incompatible, it is possible to glorify or raise the status of karma by the bliss of being. By thus glorifying the field of karma by the light of being, it becomes possible for a man to live in the field of action and simultaneously live a life of eternal freedom in bliss consciousness of absolute being. It is equally possible for man to act with full interest in the world and yet, simultaneously live God consciousness, thus bringing together the values of the absolute and the relative existence. Maharishi says that the purpose of the science of Being is to reveal this truth to man.

He further points out that the science of Being while it is perfect in its theory, is also a practical science where the results are found only when experiment is made. He says it is open to every individual to experience this state of being and create in his life a state of eternal freedom, while bringing greater success in all the fields of his activity.

How to experience being or the transcendental reality :

It has been previously said that Being, the absolute reality, lies beyond the subtlest stratum of creation, in the transcendental field of absolute existence. To experience this transcendental reality, it is necessary that our attention be led, in a concrete manner, through all the subtle states of creation, to arrive at the subtlest state. Arriving at the subtlest state and transcending that experience, we attain the state of the transcendental being.

In the field of perception, we experience both the gross and subtle things. Our sense organs are able to experience the gross objects only. Therefore, our field of experience is limited to the gross field of creation only. The subtle fields of creation are beyond the range of our common experience. We know that there are forms, much finer than our eyes can see and these can be seen through the microscope. We also know that there are waves which our ears cannot sense, and they can be heard with the help of radio. Television, helps us to hear, see and sense, the finer waves transmitted. This shows that there are subtle strata of creation in existence beyond the reach of our ordinary sense perceptions, with which we are not familiar, because our capacity of experience, is limited to the gross field only. Therefore to experience the transcendental being it is necessary to improve our faculty of experience.

A thought originates at the still depth of the mind and starts from its zero value and gradually develops. Only when it is fully developed and comes to the conscious level of the mind it is appreciated as conscious thought.

Maharishi points out that if we could improve our faculty of experience, by improving our ability to experience the thought, before it comes to the conscious level of the mind, and if this ability to perceive the thought could be so improved that is reached the very source of the thought, then, by transcending the source of the thought, we could reach the transcendental state of pure being.

This gives us a way to experience transcendental being by experiencing the finer and finer states of creation through any sense of experience, and then experience the finest stratum of experience and by transcending the finest stratum of creation, we can arrive at the state of transcendental being. It should be noted here that the state of being is of a transcendental nature and does not lie in the range of any of the senses of perception. It is only when sensory perception comes to an end, can transcendental field be reached. As long as we are experiencing though any of the senses, we are only in the relative field of experience. Therefore, Being cannot be experienced by means of any of the senses. Whatever sense of experience we adopt, we have to come to the ultimate limit of that sense perception, and then transcending that, we reach the state of consciousness, where the experiencer no longer experiences. In that state, there will be neither the experience. It is a state where the knower, known and the knowledge all become one.

It should be borne in that the term "experiencer" implies a relative state, and it is a relative field. For the experience to be, requires an object of experience. The experiencer and the object of experience belong to the relative field. In the absolute field of existence, both words lose their relevance.

Thus, when we have transcended the field of experience of the subtlest object or thought, the experiencer is in the transcendental field of being, where he is left by himself without an experience, without an object of experience and without the process of experiencing. When the subject is left without an object of experience, when he transcends the experience of the subtlest state of the object, he steps out of the field of relative experience and arrives at the transcendental state of Being. The mind is then out of the relative existence and is in the transcendental state of Being. In this state, the mind finds its own essential nature, having become being itself.

The state of Being is neither a state of objective, nor subjective existence, because both these states belong to the field of relative existence. When the subtlest state of objective experience, is transcended, the subtlest state of subjective experience is also transcended.

This state of consciousness, without an object or subject, is said to be pure consciousness or pure awareness or the state of absolute being (Turiya).

This is how, by bringing the attention to the field of the transcendent, we can contact and experience the state of Being.

Being cannot be experienced on the level of thinking, because it is beyond thought and thinking pertains to the relative field of existence. The various sense perceptions, of hearing, touching, seeing, testing and smelling all belong to the relative field of existence and have no relevance in the state of the transcendent.

It is therefore clear that the state of the transcendental Being is beyond all sense perceptions, thinking, and feeling. This state of unmanifested, absolute pure consciousness of Being, is the ultimate reality of life. It is easily experienced and attained through the system of transcendental meditation propounded by Sri Maharishi Mahesh Yogi.

Transcendental Meditation :

Maharishi defines Transcendental Meditation as the process of brining the attention of the mind, to the level of the transcendental being.

In actual practice, the way to experience the transcendental Being, is to select a proper thought, experience its subtle states until the subtlest state is experienced and transcended.

The Main Principle of Transcendental Meditation :

Being as we have seen is the state of eternal and absolute existence. The way to experience Being is to experience from the gross to the subtle states of creation until the mind arrives at the transcendent.

To get this experience, we can proceed through any sense of experience. If the sense of sight is used, we could experience gradually subtler and subtler forms, until our eyes would reach a point where they will not be able to perceive. We can close our eyes and train the inner eye — the eye of the mind, to perceive the object from the point at which we fail to perceive it through our open eyes. We would then be seeing mentally the image of the object and, if we could continue experiencing the finer and finer fields of that mental image, we would be arriving at the finest state of the image and then by transcending it we would reach the state of Being. Likewise through any sense of experience we could start experiencing the object, and eventually arrive at the transcendental state of Being.

In a similar way by employing the medium of a thought we could go on experiencing subtle state of thinking and transcending the subtlest state of thinking, we are sure to arrive at the transcendental state of Being.

Thinking in itself is the subtle state of speech. When we speak, our words are audible to the ears, but if we do not speak, the words do not become perceptible to the organ of hearing. But when we think, the subtle state of speech becomes audible to the inner ear the ear of the mind. Thus we find that thought is a subtle form of sound. Thought, which is a subtle form of sound, can be heard through the inner ear— the ear of the mind.

Sri Maharishi gives the analogy of the ocean to explain the phenomenon of thought. The thought starts from the deepest level of consciousness, from the deepest level of the ocean of mind as a bubble starts at the bottom of the sea. The bubble becomes bigger as it rises and when it comes to the surface of the water, it is perceived as a bubble. Mind is like an ocean and as in the ocean, the surface layers are active, in the form of waves, and the deeper levels are silent. The surface levels of the mind are actively functioning and the deeper levels are calm and silent. The surface functioning level of the ocean of mind is said to be the conscious mind. Any thought on the surface level is consciously reconsised. The level on the ocean of mind, where the thoughts appear and are appreciated, is the conscious level of the mind.

Any thought originating at the deepest level of consciousness, travels the whole range of the depth of the mind and finally reaches the conscious level and appears as conscious thought. It is only when the thought reaches the conscious level, it is consciously appreciated as thought. The rest of the many states of the development of thought are not appreciated. That is why we say for all practical purposes, the deeper levels of the ocean of consciousness are as though silent. We also know that at the deepest level of consciousness, where the thought originates, is the field of pure consciousness, or, the field of the transcendental Being. If the bubble of thought could be consciously appreciated at all levels below the level of the conscious mind, and at the source, and if it were possible to transcend that experience at the source of the thought, then the mind would giant he state of transcendental consciousness. It would then be possible to bring within the range of the conscious mind, the entire range, within which, the development of thought takes place, right from the point of origin of thought, to the surface level of conscious mind. The power of the conscious mind would then be increased many fold. This expansion of the conscious capacity of the mind will be on the mental level, on the way to experience Being.

Technique of Transcendental Meditation :

Thought bubbles are produced one after the other in a stream. In Transcendental Meditation, the mind is trained to experience the oncoming bubbles in the earlier and earlier stages of their development. The attention of the mind thus traverses the subtler and subtler stage of thought development, till it reaches the subtlest stage of thought. The attention traverses the whole depth of the mind, and reaches the source of creative intelligence in man. The source of thought thus comes within the scope of the conscious mind. When the conscious mind transcends the subtlest state of thought of relative experience, it arrives at the state of transcendental Being, the source of pure consciousness, or self awareness.

This is how, in a systematic manner the conscious mind is led on, step by step, to the direct experience of transcendental absolute Being.

Increasing charm on the path of transcending :

Maharishi mentions the most important aspect in Transcendental Meditation, which forms the basis of his theory of transcendence. He speaks of the increasing charm on the path of transcending. He says the natural tendency of the mind is to be attracted to a field of greater happiness. Because in the practice of Transcendental

Meditation, the mind is set on its way to transcending and experiencing transcendental absolute Being, and because the nature of transcendental Being is bliss consciousness, the conscious mind finds that the path is increasingly, attractive and alluring, as it advances in the direction of bliss. Maharishi gives the example of a light becoming dim and faint as we go away from its source, while the intensity increases as we proceed towards the source. In a similar manner when the mind goes in the direction of the absolute bliss of the transcendental Being, it finds increasing charm at every step of its march. The mind is therefore automatically led on and on, towards transcendental Being until it transcends and attains the state of the transcendental Being.

Increased conscious Capacity of the mind :

Maharishi speaks about the increased conscious capacity of the mind which results in Transcendental Meditation. On the path to experience transcendental Being, the conscious mind traverses the entire range of thought up to the source. Thereby, the conscious capacity of the mind is enlarged, and the whole ocean of the mind becomes capable of becoming conscious. The full mental potential of the mind is thus unfolded and the conscious capacity enlarged to the maximum limit.

Importance of a proper thought :

The thought selected for Transcendental Meditation should be a proper thought. By a proper thought is meant, that it should be harmonious in its nature. Every thought and every spoken word, has some influence on the thinker and on his surroundings. The whole universe is influenced by every thought, word, and action of particular about the quality of thought that the creates in his mind. The thought should not be detrimental to the thinker and to the rest of the universe. It should be useful to the thinker and to the world at large. Maharishi says that each personality has its own quality and depending upon this, each man should select for himself a special quality of thought whose physical influence will be good and useful to himself and will do good to the world at large.

It is said that the influence of a spoken word is carried by the waves of vibration, set up in the atmosphere and it does not depend upon the meaning of the word. It depends upon the quality of vibration set forth by the spoken word. To produce vibrations of good quality which will have an influence of harmony and happiness, the quality of vibrations produced should correspond to that of the individual. Individuals differ in the quality of vibrations produced by them, and these constitute their individual personalities. Therefore the selection of a proper thought for a particular individual becomes all the more difficult. Another important factor to be considered, is the power of the thought which increases when the thought is appreciated at the subtle stage of development. The power is greater in the subtle strata of creation than in the gross. When we enter into the subtler states of a thought, and we begin to appreciate its finer levels, the power of the thought is much greater than its power of the thought is much greater than its power on the common level of the conscious mind. Maharishi says, that, on the common level of the conscious mind. Maharishi says, that, bearing this in mind, before starting the practice of Transcendental Meditation, a proper quality of sound should be selected. Since the consideration of an action and its influence is highly complicated, the selection of a proper thought producing favourable results for the doer and the surroundings becomes important. Maharishi mentions that the problem of selecting a proper thought for the daily practice of Transcendental Meditation cannot be decided by any, and every individual on his own. It can only be done by trained teachers of Transcendental Meditation who, Maharishi says, are specially trained for the purpose and are available at all centers of the spiritual regeneration movement, in almost every country of the world.

Necessity of personal guidance :

It is further pointed out by Sri Maharishi that, by necessity, the practice of Transcendental Meditation should be verbally taught. It cannot be learnt through a book, because it involves not only telling an aspirant how to experience the subtle states of thinking, but also to find out what the aspirant actually experiences when he proceeds on that path. Thought by itself, is a very abstract experience for a common man, and for an ordinary person to experience the finer state of that abstract experience, seems to be an impossible task, because, the mind of an ordinary man is only accustomed to experience gross and concrete objects. The experiences on the path of Transcendental Meditation being very subtle, the experiencer himself often is not certain that he is experiencing anything, because the moment he begins to experience the subtle state of thought, he finds himself drifting away to nothingness. For a beginner, it takes sometime before he is able to explain his experience of the subtle state of thought. Therefore, it is not possible to put into writing, how the mind passes through the experiences of the subtle state of thought. Maharishi, therefore points out that the practice of Transcendental Meditation should always be imparted by the expert teachers of Transcendental Meditation, who have been properly trained to impart it, and who have been trained to check the experiences. The checking of experience according to Maharishi is a vital factor in the practice of Transcendental Meditation and it can only be done by personal instruction from expert teachers and cannot be done through books. He further says that the practice of Transcendental Meditation must result in all good in life, and since it is by nature delicate and therefore highly technical, the only method of imparting, has to be by personal instructions and guidance so as to make the way smooth and easy.

How to live Being or the Transcendental reality in actual life :

Next Maharishi deals with the question how we should live transcendental reality in actual life. He explains Being or transcendental reality, as not smoothing lying outside of us. It cannot be brought, from somewhere outside and lived. Being is existence, our own self. It is the life of everything that exists. It is the all pervading omnipresent state of absolute consciousness. To live it, the conscious mind has to get itself familiar with it. It should become acquainted with it as previously described under the heading "how to experience being or, the transcendental reality". It has been previously described under Transcendental Meditation. In Transcendental Meditation when the conscious mind transcends the subtlest state of thinking and arrives at the transcendental state of Being, there is no experience, as the whole field of relativity has been transcended. It is just the state of transcendence, the state of existence, the state of pure consciousness.

From this state of pure Being, the mind comes back again to experience thought in the relative world. Through the regular practice of Transcendental Meditation and the mind constantly going, into the field of the transcendental reality and coming back to the field of relativity, familiarity of the mind with the essential nature of Being deepens. The mind becomes gradually more aware of its own essential nature. With more and more practice of transcendental meditation, Maharishi says, the ability of the mind to maintain its essential nature, while experiencing the objects through the senses increases. When this happens, the mind and its essential nature, the state of the transcendental Being become one. The mind then becomes capable of retaining its essential nature-being-even while it is engaged in thought, speech or action. To achieve such a state of mind, according to Maharishi, two things are said to be necessary. One is the regular practice of Transcendental Meditation. The other, and equally important, for the rapid achievement of the desired goal, is that the mind. When it comes out after meditation to engage itself in the field of activity, should not be strained. On this point he emphasizes that the whole field of activity should be properly planned and attended to, and all action performed, but the mind should not be overtaxed. Everything should be done in an easy and comfortable way. This precaution of taking life naturally and easily is said to be very important, according to Maharishi, for the quick infusion of Being into the nature of the active mind.

When the conscious mind transcends and gains the state of pure Being, it becomes one hundred percent of the state of being. In that state the mind loses its individuality and becomes cosmic mind; it becomes omnipresent and gains the state of pure, eternal existence. In the transcendental state, it loses its capacity to experience. In this state the mind does not exists, but it becomes existence itself.

When the mind comes back into the field of relative life it once again gains its individuality, but it also seems to retain some of the great unbounded, universal, oneness which it had just attained. With continued practice of Transcendental Meditation, attained. With continued practice of Transcendental Meditation, it is able to retain more and more of that experience in the activity of daily life. It is further said by Maharishi, that any engagement of the mind in the field of activity is naturally a strain for the essential nature of the mind. But if the mind engages itself in the activity in an easy unstrained, simple and natural manner, the infusion of the nature of Being into the nature of the mind becomes greater and the infusion is retained for sometime. If on the other hand, the mind is trained in the course of its activity, the infusion of being into the nature of the mind becomes less effective. It is therefore, suggested that one engages in the field of activity in a natural and normal manner, so that, the activity itself, serves as a means to culture the mind to be in the state of Being.

It has been found therefore that the regular practice of Transcendental Meditation along with a life of regulated activity, is a direct way of living Being, or a short cut, for creating a state of consciousness, whereby absolute Being and the relative field of life are both lived simultaneously without either, being a barrier to the other.

Therefore, by the system of Transcendental Meditation, it is possible and easy for everyone, to cultivate the state of cosmic consciousness in which Being is lived along with the values of relative life.

It has been observed that those who take up to the practice of Transcendental Meditation, feel more energy, greater clarity of mind and better health. They become more efficient and more energetic in all the activities of their lives. Maharishi sounds a note of warning against overworking as a result of increased efficiency, in their mental and physical activities. He urges the practitioners not to blow themselves up into activity on account of their increased efficiency and energy, to such an extent, that they become exhausted and find no time for meditation.

Maharishi here gives the example of the tree, where the root receives water and the tree becomes green and more vital, for the purpose of growing more. But, if the activity of growing, is cherished by the tree to such an extent, that it has no time to draw in the water from the root, then the very basis of the growth is lost.

With the regular practice of Transcendental Meditation, the nature of the mind gets infused with the nature of Being. This results in the rejuvenation of personality, clear thinking and greater energy and, this is a very delicate process. Maharishi points out that such rejuvenation of the personality is on the level of Being, the very existence f the individual. It is never on the level of the conscious mind.

Therefore, the aspirants are cautioned not to expect to feel Being on the level of the conscious mind. Whatever influence of Transcendental Meditation there is, takes place in the field of Being and is beyond all relative phenomena, and hence, beyond the purview of the conscious mind and therefore, the conscious mind cannot feel it. To make this point clear, Maharishi cites the example of a tree receiving water at its root, and consequently all the parts of the tree like branches, leaves etc., automatically receiving nourishment and flourishing. No other part of the tree knows or experiences the process of the root receiving the water. But its influence is seen in the increasing freshness of all the parts of the tree. It may be that the leaf of the tree may argue that it is feeling better, but does not feel that it is receiving any nourishment. The constitution of the leaf has been that it naturally received life energy from the roots, but it cannot feel the actual process of the nourishment of the sap coming to it. It does not recognize that this is happening, but what is happening to it is appreciated, however, by all those who have seen the leaf drying up, but now see, that it is becoming fresh and is flourishing. Similarly when one practices Transcendental Meditation, one experiences increased energy and clarity of mind, but one does not experience the actual process of the infusion of Being, into the nature of the mind. Maharishi points out that the whole process is silent on the level of pure Being. Whatever experiences one has during meditation, they are just relative states of the medium of meditation. During meditation, these states become finer and finer until, eventually, nothing is left of the medium and the mind is left all by itself in the state of pure consciousness. With regular practice of Transcendental Meditation one does succeed in living being. The infusion of the nature of Being into the nature of the mind takes place at the level of Being, which is the very nature of the mind, and cannot be felt, but it can only be lived. Living being cannot be described, neither can it be intellectually conceived. It can only be lived and experienced. Maharishi gives the example of a person who is eating and enjoying the taste. He cannot adequately describe the taste even though he was able to taste the food.

Maharishi mentions certain aspects of meditation, which may be helpful to the practitioners of Transcendental Meditation, in achieving results. (1) Being or the transcendental reality is very well lived in life, and is a state of experience which cannot be precisely described. (2) In the beginning of the practice of meditation, the nature of Being is very delicately impressed upon the nature of the mind. (3) As the practice is continued, it (being) becomes more and more deeply infused in the nature of the mind. Eventually the infusion of Being into the nature of mind becomes so deep, significant, and unshakable that Being is lived all the time through all the experiences of the wakeful, dreaming, and deep sleep states. (4) Then one lives in a state of eternal freedom while being engaged actively, in the life of relative experience.

Advantages of the experience of Being :

Maharishi cites the several advantages of the experience of absolute being, through the practice of Transcendental Meditation. The advantages are (1) it influences the life of the individual on all levels of his activity, to such a great degree that the whole life of the individual is transformed to a value, beyond the human mind's imagination. (2) When the mortal man's life comes in contact with the cosmic life of absolute Being of eternal status, there will open out the possibilities for the individual, to function with the whole of his potential and to remain in tune with the center of creative intelligence of absolute being. (3) The experience of being permits one to live life in its full status and significance. It leads man to live the normal life of man in cosmic consciousness. Man lives a life in peace, through elimination of fear, tension and suffering. (4) The direct experience of the transcendental state of Being enables man to use his full potential and to make the full use of his surroundings and of the almighty power of nature. The material and the spiritual values of life are brought into harmony and this makes it possible for man to live life in eternal freedom, while he still accomplishes the maximum in the material field. Being begins to be lived in all phases of life, the body, mind nervous system, action, speech, thought, breath, behaviour and surroundings. (5) When being is brought to the level of the individual mind it provides the key to clear, purposeful, and fruitful thinking. It brings forth self confidence and leads the individual to increase efficiency, in all his undertakings. (6) Transcendental Meditation fulfills man's yearning for a religious life, provides the true fulfillment of psychology and philosophy, and leads to God realization.

PART II

Life, and level of Being affecting various aspects of life

Life :

It has been previously stated that Being—is the field of unlimited unbounded eternal life, pure intelligence, pure existence, the absolute.

Maharishi describes life as the expression of Divinity. It is the stream of eternal being. He says "Life is absolute in bliss consciousness and relative in the variety of phenomenal joy" (Page 61—Science of being and Art of Living—T.M). Thus life is essentially being. In its essential nature life is unbounded eternal ocean of Being.

Life eternally remaining absolute being, is found in different qualities, forms and phenomena of the Divine creation. It is composed of different levels of understanding, different levels of intelligence and creativity, and different levels of happiness.

Maharishi gives the example of a tree to illustrate what life is. All the outer aspects of the tree comprising trunk, branches, leaves, flowers and fruits, together with the various aspects of the inner root, go to make up the whole life of the tree. If we look more closely into the life of the tree we find that although the root is the basis of the outer tree, it has no absolute independent status. The root functions on account of the nourishment or sap, which comes from the area outside the root itself. This sap is the essence of the entire tree. It makes the root, and passing through the root, gives rise to the various aspects of the tree.

It is thus seen that the tree in essence is nothing but the nourishment that comes from outside the boundary of the individual tree. The tree is obviously limited within the bounds of the root, and the outer tree, but its basis is outside these bounds.

This basis of life is of transcendental nature; it transcends the boundaries of the inner and outer tree. It is the field of essential constituent of life. Similarly, the life of man or any individual life in creation has three aspects: the outer, the inner and the transcendental. The outer aspects of life is the body; the inner is the subjective aspects of the personality which is concerned with the process of experience and action; and the transcendental aspect is unmanifested absolute Being. It manifests as the ego, intellect, mind, senses and prana, and all these subtle states of life make up the inner man, or the subject within, the subjective aspect of life. The subjective aspect of life differs from the objective aspect of life, which is the body in all its various attributes.

Hence, when we consider life, we have to consider it in all its phases. Thus, life in its full scope has three aspects. The objective aspect, the subjective aspect and the transcendental aspect. This is the life in its totality.

Purpose of life:

Maharishi next speaks about the purpose of life. He mentions the purpose of life as the expansion of happiness. This is secured by the process of the cosmos. Evolution of the cosmos is served by the evolution of the individual life. If one is not constantly developing his intelligence, power, creativity, peace and happiness, he has not served the purpose of life. Life is not meant to be lived in dullness, idleness and suffering and these are contrary to the essential nature of life, says Maharishi.

It is found that man's nervous system is the most highly evolved system in creation. Speaking on this aspect, Maharishi says, "Therefore the scope of evolution in case of man is unlimited., in this life". (Page 64 Science of Being and Art of Living T.M.). the nervous system in case of man is found to be complete nervous system and has developed to the extent, that, through proper activity, man can contract absolute bliss and develop creativity, intelligence, power and energy. Man is born to live a perfect life, covering all the values of the transcendental absolute divine, of unlimited energy, intelligence power, peace and bliss, along with the unlimited values of the world of multiplicity, in the diverse relative existence. Say, Maharishi, "Man's life is to cultivate and give—cultivate the divine power, the divine intelligence, happiness and abundance, and give it out to all of creation. This is the high purpose of the life of man and it is fortunate to find that every man is capable of reaching this by improving the conscious capacity of his mind and consciously contacting the field of the absolute, energy, peace, happiness and abundance of the eternal, divine consciousness". (Page 65, Science of Being and Art of Living—T.M.).

Every man is capable of living a life of full values. If one fails to live it, Maharishi says, it is a disgrace to oneself and an abuse of the glory of almighty God, within and above us. Maharishi, therefore, in his message invites every man on earth to start picking up the divine consciousness of the absolute and bring it out through all his activity, into the world of variety and thereby enjoy the happiness for himself, and project it for all others to enjoy as well. All ills and sufferings in human life can be traced to the lack of knowledge to dive within oneself, to unfold the divine glory present within. Without attaining the state of divine consciousness, man is found lacking in energy, intelligence and clear thinking. He becomes tired, worried, tense and anxious.

With all its advances in science and technology, modern scientific age, instead of making life easy and comfortable for man, is found to increase tension. The individual finds himself an anxious and worried man. It is because, the individuals have no way of improving their ability and efficiency, through the contact with the fields of greater energy and intelligence lying within themselves. It is only necessary that the individual should contact consciously that field of inner life and profit by it. In the face of stiff competition in modern society, a man has to work hard, and when activity increases, he finds himself unable to cope with the increased pressure and life's demands. His efficiency declines and he does not find enough energy to cope with the increased activity. This results in tensions and strains. As his activity increases, man should be able to produce more energy and greater intelligence within himself, to cope with the increased demands of his activity. This can be done only, by contacting the divine within oneself and drawing more energy and greater intelligence from the great absolute field of unbounded energy, intelligence and creativity. Which exists within himself. It is only to achieve this objective that Maharishi has placed before the world his system of Transcendental Meditation.

Normal Life of Man :

It has been previously stated that life has two aspects, the relative and the absolute. Therefore, normal life should mean that both these aspects are lived and enjoyed in a natural way, to fulfill the overall purpose of life.

A Man is said to live a normal life, when he lives the full values of the material field of the world, supplemented by the eternal freedom in God consciousness. Cosmic consciousness is said to be the normal consciousness of human beings.

The ability of living the transcendental state of Being, along with the experiences of transitory nature of relative existence is the normal capacity of human life. This is brought about by the practice of Transcendental Meditation, as previously described. It unfolds the divine in man and brings human consciousness to the high pedestal of God consciousness. It brings life to a state of eternal freedom, supplementing it with unlimited creative energy and harmonizing the abstract absolute values of the divine being, with the concrete physical material values of day to day human life.

Individual and cosmic Life :

It has been previously mentioned that life has two aspects the absolute and the relative. The relative aspect of life is only the expression of the absolute phase of life, which is the omnipresent, unlimited, unbounded, ocean of pure consciousness or eternal existence.

This unbounded ocean of eternal existence is said to be cosmic life and its expression in the relative field is called individual life.

Individual life is said to be the expression of cosmic life, just as a wave is the expression of the ocean. The ocean while remaining the same, gets its expression in the form of waves and the ocean is affected by every wave and its activity.

The Universe reacts to individual action :

The wave of individual life on account of its activity produces an influence which is felt in all fields of the cosmos. Life is one continuous and homogenous whole, from which the waves of individual life arise, without in any way breaking the continuity and the all pervading status of eternal absolute Being.

It is found that the life of every cell in the human body influences the whole life of man. If something happens to one cell in one tissue of the body, the entire body reacts to it. In a similar manner the whole universe reacts to individual action.

We, through every thought word and action, are producing an influence affecting our surroundings. Through every thing we do, we are producing vibrations in the atmosphere, waves of activity, are set up inside our individual system, and are emitted from the body to reach all strata of the atmosphere. In recent times, the devices set up in satellites and other bodies orbiting the far off planets receive commands from earth and send back information from great distances. All these establish that life is one continuous whole, and our actions produce reactions in the unlimited space field, beyond our immediate surroundings. Every thing in the universe is therefore constantly influencing every other things.

This only shows how dependent, and at the same time how powerful, is the life of the individual. One may not be aware of the influence he is producing in the surroundings, but the influence is produced nonetheless. A man having a kind and compassionate nature will produce a good influence on others and in the vicinity. If we enter the home of a friend and a virtuous man we feel elated and experience a sense of joy. If he is a man of good intentions, good thought and good actions, then he certainly creates a very good atmosphere around him. We have seen teachers of humanity, who are sincere and virtuous people and who are motivated with a sense of service to the cause of the poor and the down-trodden, carry with them that influence of harmony, peace and happiness, attracting large sections of people to the cause that they have exposed. Maharishi points out, that, in the relative fields of life in the cosmos, the influence of each aspect of life on every other aspect of life, being so complex and diverse, it is very important that a situation should somehow be created in the world that every man is a righteous man. He therefore exhorts that every man should be compassionate, loving and helpful man. His every thought, should be kind, loving and virtuous, so that he produces a good influence on the thinker and the surroundings and in the universe.

Everyone should know that he is a part of the whole life of the whole life of the universe. His relationship to the universal life is, what the life of a cell is to the life of the whole body. If therefore, every cell is not alert, energetic and healthy, the body as a whole begins to suffer. It is therefore, necessary that the individual be healthy, virtuous, good and right in his every thought, word and deed, so that the life of the whole universe gets a favourable influence from every action of the individual. In return, the universe reacts favourably to the individual action.

In view of this understanding of the individual and his influence on the cosmos, it becomes highly important that every individual should strive to develop his consciousness in such a way, that he is always right and good. He should, by his thought, word and action, create life supporting and life sustaining influences for himself and for the whole creation. Maharishi says that this may be created by each individual for himself by transforming the nature of his mind in such a way and in such a manner that, by nature, the mind picks up only right thought and engages itself in right speech and action.

Maharishi further points out that every man has to rise to this state by himself, and that nobody else could possible raise the standard of another man's consciousness. Even though some help by way of information and guidance by those who know the way, could be offered to others, the responsibility of raising one's consciousness entirely lies in oneself. Every one has to work out his own destiny. On this aspect Maharishi makes and appeal, 'If all those to whom such information comes through this book would inform their neighbours, associates and circles of friends that there is a way to improve the consciousness of the individual and transform one's nature in a way which will make the individual spontaneously good for his own benefit and for that of all creation, it would be a great help to humanity. There is a very great responsibility on every individual". (Page 73—Science of Being and Art of Living—TM. By Shri Maharishi Mahesh Yogi).

We have seen previously how the regular practice of Transcendental Meditation raises the consciousness of the individual, to the level of the state of Being. This automatically places the nature of the mind in such a manner that the individual will be naturally doing good actions, for his own benefit, and for the benefit of the entire creation.]

Art of Living :

Maharishi defines "ART" as the graceful and skillful method of accomplishment. The art of living involves that a man should live the full values of life. He should accomplish the maximum in the world. At the same time, he should live a life of eternal freedom, in God consciousness.

It has been stated earlier that the sap is the basis of the root and the entire tree. The root lies between the transcendental area of the tree, and the outer tree. In a similar manner the subjective aspect of life which consists of the inner man (ego, mind and senses) lies between the transcendental Being (the basis of our life) and the outer gross field of objective existence.

The art of living requires that the mind should draw the power of Being and pass it on to the body and surroundings. But taking the example of the tree, it is seen that for the efficient growth of the tree to maturity, the root should draw efficiently the proper nourishment required, from the surroundings and give it out to all the different aspects of the outer tree. This analogy helps us to understand what is meant by the "Art of living". In a similar manner the inner man, or the subjective aspect of man should absorb the value of the transcendental absolute state of life, and give it out to the outer gross relative state of life, thereby, enriching every aspect of life and supplementing it with the power of absolute Being. The individual creative energy is thereby supplemented by the unlimited, unbounded creative energy of cosmic Being. For this to happen, the mind should be in constant communion with the absolute state of life, so that when the mind is thinking acting or experiencing, it is never away from the influence of eternal absolute Being.

It is therefore necessary that the mind should cultivate within itself, the eternal absolute state of Being. For, without constant and continuous infusion of the absolute, into the very nature of the mind, the mind can never be, all comprehensive and all powerful.

As Maharishi points out, it is necessary that the individual mind should bring out the bliss of absolute Being and remain saturated with that bliss, while it experiences things in the outside relative field of life. Or, otherwise, nothing that is experienced by the mind will ever bring contentment to it. Mind's nature is such, that is will always be searching for greater happiness. It is only when the mind is saturated with the bliss of absolute being, that it derives joy from the variety of multiple creating, and it is only then, that it remains well established in contentment and fully enjoys the world of variety in relative creation.

On the other hand, a mind without the basis of the bliss of unity within, gets tossed about from one point to another, in search of happiness, having no stable status of its own.

It is therefore necessary, for the experiences in life, to be of maximum charm and joy and of real value in the world of variety, that the bliss of absolute being should remain infused into the very nature of the mind.

The world of variety can be enjoyed only, when the mind has gained an unshakable status in the bliss of absolute Being. The 'Art of living' therefore requires that, for life to be lived in all its values, the subjective aspect of life be infused with the bliss and power of Being. It is only then, that all aspects of life will be glorified and man lives his full potential.

Man's full potential :

The full potential of man means that, on all levels of life, physical, mental, and spiritual, one should live to one's full capacity. On the physical level, it means man should have a healthy body, in which all the limbs and the nervous system are functioning normally. They should be in co-ordination with each other. One the mental plane of life, it means that the individual should be able to make use of his full mental capacity. On the spiritual plane of life, man should be able to live the full value of spiritual Being, in all fields of daily life.

We have seen under Transcendental Meditation that the human mind has the ability to take its consciousness to the field of the transcendental absolute divine Being. This shows that the whole range of creation and the field of the ultimate creator, almighty universal Being, is capable of coming within the scope of human life. Hence the full potential of man, is the full cosmic life open to each individual. Man can achieve as his full potential, the unlimited potential of universal Being. Therefore, a normal human life means, living a life of divine consciousness, and a normal human mind means that the mind functions on human levels, but, at the same time it retains the status of universal cosmic mind. It will be a cosmically conscious mind.

The practice of Transcendental Meditation furnishes a direct and simple techniques, for beginning to express one's full potential in a natural way, whereby the divine in man is unfolded and the human consciousness is brought to the level of God consciousness. It brings life to a state of eternal freedom, supplementing it, with unlimited creative energy. It harmonises the abstract absolute values of the divine Being, with the concrete physical material values of day-to-day activities of human life. Hence, everyman should strive to be a cosmically conscious man, living with his mind, infused with the value of the absolute Being, and possessing, to the maximum, the power, energy peace and happiness in the relative field, instead of remaining in a dull, weak and powerless state.

How to use one's full potential :

To use one's full potential in life, it is necessary that life as a whole, should have a solid basis for itself, without a strong basis, life would just be as unstable, as a building without a strong foundation.

It is seen that life in this relative stages is ever changing. The ever changing phases of life leave no stable status of life. Maharishi says that in order to be able to use one's full potential, the first step is to infuse stability into the ever changing phases of relative life.

But stability belongs to the absolute state. Stability is an attribute, of that factor of life which never changes. That which never changes is the truth of life, the ultimate reality, the eternal Being. Life then, in its absolute state alone possesses stability. When stability is gained by the mind, and retained through all the mind's activity of experience and action, the whole field of activity is enriched by the power of the never changing absolute Being.

Maharishi points out that, to use one's full potential, the mind should be taken to the field of absolute Being, before it is brought out, to face the gross aspect of the relative fields of life. This is done, by the simple technique of bringing the mind to the field of Being in a simple and effective way, through the regular and systematic practice of Transcendental Meditation.

How to make full use of the surroundings :

According to Maharishi, surroundings are of two types. There are those, that are consciously created and those, that are created, without the individual's conscious knowledge, as the result of his own thought, speech, or action.

The unintentional creation of the surroundings is said to be, in accordance with the theory of Karma. The present surroundings are the result of something we have done in the past. Our present intentions and efforts have materialized due to the influence of the past. Therefore, it can be said that the surroundings are, not only the result of our past, but the result of a combination of past and present. Such is the life of man in the present.

It is natural that one receives what he is in position to give. The mother gives to the child her love and in return, she receives abundance of love from the child. That action and reaction are equal, is a scientifically established truth. If you react to someone in a certain way, he will react to you in a similar way. If you are open with some one, he will be open with you. The law of nature is, as you sow, so you reap. If you want kindness and sympathy from some one, be kind and sympathetic to him. If you are sincere in giving, you will receive it many fold. If you want the surroundings to react to you in a particular way, your behaviour toward the surroundings must be in accordance with that. This is the fundamental principle making the best use of the surroundings. Therefore, if we want to receive the maximum at all times, we must have an attitude of giving. The law of nature is "If you want to receive, you must give".

Maharishi further says that the law of nature is inexorable. The reaction will come. If you hurt someone, even if he himself does not hurt you, other agencies of nature will bring the reaction to you. If you are kind to him, the surroundings will be kind to you.

If you forgive, all nature enjoys your action and returns joy to you. Forgiveness, tolerance, purity of heart, sincerity, love and kindness are the virtues from which to enjoy and make full use of the surroundings, on the fundamental principle of giving.

Hence in all walks of life, under all circumstances, in all surroundings, animate or inanimate, living or non-living, we should have a very loving, kind and sympathetic temperament in the inner core of our heart. Our outward behaviour must be an expression of this inner attitude.

This is the fundamental technique of making full use of the surroundings. It means you derive maximum advantage from the surroundings. You enjoy the surroundings, and will make them do the most for you, only, if you are established in loving kindness and sympathy for them.

Surroundings may also be considered from a different view point—the immediate surroundings and the surroundings the are distant and remote. The immediate surroundings that are near to us are directly affected by our behaviour, speech and action, in relation to them. But the surroundings that are remote from us are mostly reacting to our feelings and thoughts. For example, if you are in India and you have a son, or a friend, in America, his feeling of heart and mind will be according to the feeling of your heart and your mind.

It is said that thought waves are much more powerful than the waves of speech and action. We are creating through our every thought, word and action, some wave in the atmosphere, but thought waves are especially penetrating. If we are joyful, happy, and full of kindness and live, for the whole world, we receive love from every quarter. If we want to make use to the best advantage of the surroundings, whether they are near or remote from us, the golden rule is that at the center of our being, heart and mind, we should possess, kind, loving, forgiving and sympathetic thoughts for all surroundings. If one follows throughout his life the principle—"Give, if you want to receive"- there will be no dearth for the receiving and the receiving will be equal to, or more than, what is given, because, receiving rebounds from many parts of the surroundings.

Maharishi says, "If you cultivate within yourself a natural state of kindness, compassion, love and forgiveness, you will receive a thousand fold reward from the surroundings. In order to make full use of the surroundings, it is necessary to develop these qualities within yourself to the fullest capacity: these are merely the potentialities that are within you. If one is able to rise to this full value of human life, one may receive the maximum possible and make full use of the surroundings to his own best advantage". (Page-89 science of and Art of Living—TM).

The regular practice of Transcendental Meditation brings our all the inner mental potentialities and the inner divine nature. One gains the direct experience of bliss consciousness and fullness of life. All types of surroundings being to react in a favourable way, and will offer the best use of their values.

By setting ourselves in tune with nature, by raising the consciousness to the level of the transcendental pure consciousness, we can enter the realm of all harmony, peace and happiness which only lies in the eternal status of the absolute. It is only then, will it be possible for us to make the full use of the surroundings at all levels.

Maharishi here makes an important observation that changing the surroundings, or making full use of them will not be possible by either force, or moral pressure, or suggestion.

On the attempt of modern psychology, to reconcile the surroundings of a man, by the system of improving his relationship through suggestion and psychological training, the says "Trying to build up human life purely on the consideration of the surface of psychology can amuse the intellect of some ignorant people, but it cannot serve the real purpose of life". He further continues, "If a petal of a flower starts to wither, a skilled gardener does not water the petal, he waters the root. If a relationship begins to create tension, very little can be gained by trying to reconcile the parties by suggestion on the surface. Bad relationships should be handled by improving the quality of heart and mind of both the parties." (Page 91 — Science of Being and Art of Living — TM).

Maharishi quote by an example how quickly, the conscious capacity of the mind is improved by the practice of Transcendental Meditation. We have seen in the world that, if someone feels sad by some tragedy, people try to console him by suggestions and goodwill. But it is hard for him to assemble in his mind, all the suggestions and goodwill, with which others try to console him. But, if he starts the practice of Transcendental Meditation, within ten minutes, he finds mind calming down, doubts beginning to be dispelled from inside, the tension beginning to resolve, and compassion beginning to glow.

After Transcendental Meditation, he is able to view the situation from an enlarged consciousness and vision. Immediately he becomes forging and tolerant, about the same thing, which was a terrible problem, a few minutes before. The tragedy is the same, the circumstances are the same. At one moment, he does not derive the advantage and is miserable from the surroundings. At the next moment, due to the raising of his consciousness, through the method of Transcendental Meditation, he begins to appreciate the surroundings, and to develop maximum advantage for himself and others.

Hence, in order to be able to make full use of the surroundings, it is first necessary to raise one's consciousness through the regular practice of Transcendental Meditation; all the surroundings and circumstances will, by nature be helpful and be fully used to the best advantage of oneself, and all others.

How to make full use of the almighty power of nature :

We have seen previously that it lies within the capacity of each individual, to contact and I live absolute Being in his day-to-day life by a technique which is simple and easy for him to do.

By the regular practice of Transcendental Meditation it is possible for man to have the value of transcendental Being, infused into the very nature of the mind, whether the mind is in the wakeful, dreaming, or deep sleep states. Thereby, man has naturally placed himself on the level of Being, which is the basic foundation for all the laws of nature to function. Maharishi says, man placed in this position, is in tune with all the laws of nature and he is naturally able to use the almighty power of nature.

This may look strange, as Maharishi points out, for those who have not understood the value of Being, and who have not themselves started the practice of Transcendental Meditation, that man could ever place himself in such a position. Where he will be using the power of nature. It is much beyond their imagination. Further, man is engrossed with the complexities and unsolved problems of every day life, and is gripped with the tension of day to day activities. For such a man, the possibility that the could place himself in a position, where he will be naturally using the almighty power of nature may look like a fantastic notion, having no bearing on practical life. But with all sincerity and openness at his command, Maharishi records, and brings home to the innocent, ignorant, simple and suffering people of the world, that they are in a position, to rise above all miseries and tensions of life and to make all their circumstances favourable to themselves, and agreeable to all the evolution possible for their lives.

He further mentions that one has to completely put oneself, in the hands of the almighty power of nature, to derive the great strength needed fir making use of the almighty power of nature. It one is able to submit oneself to nature, then nature will react to his needs. Almighty nature is all powerful, and all kind and loving, and all the laws of nature are for the creation and evolution of all the beings and creatures of the entire cosmos.

It is not possible for the human intellect to understand all the complexities of the laws of nature, and their working, so as to put oneself in accordance with the natural flow of evolution governed by nature. The constant and eternal process of creation and evolution of the multiple variety of creation, is highly complex and diversified in its nature. None other than Almighty intelligence alone, could set the whole process of this vast creation in the functioning order. It is not possible for the human intellect to go into all the depths of the complexity and variety of the circumstances existing in the vast span of the universe. Maharshi points out, that there is one factor alone in the entire field of creation, on which, one could base an attempt to meet the order of the laws of nature. It is the factor that all the laws of nature are functioning in the direction of evolution. It is found that nature flows in one way and takes every thing on to higher evolution. The individual can consciously put himself in tune with this one way flow of nature, and permit nature to work on him. Then the natural flow of evolution of the individual will be in consonance with the purpose of cosmic evolution.

Maharishi points out that such a situation has been rendered possible, by the great tradition of the Yogis of India and by the blessings of his Guru Shri Guru Dev. The ushering in, at the present age, of the system of Transcendental Meditation by Shri Maharishi Mahesh Yogi has brought forth a simple technique whereby one's consciousness could be easily placed on the level of Being, which is the level of the natural flow of evolution, the basic plane on which all the laws of nature function. It is only when the individual places his consciousness on that level, it is possible to put one's whole life in tune with the level of the functioning of the almighty power of nature.

It is by submitting oneself in this manner to the almighty power of Mother Nature, that one is said to become the loving submissive, and obedient child of nature, enjoying all the powers of the divine. This is said to be the simple way of making use of the almighty power of nature. Speaking about this, Maharishi says, "Life finds its fulfillment in submission, surrender, devotion, losing oneself, and gaining the power of almighty". (Page 95 — Science of Being and Art of Living—TM).

From here, it is said, originates the ideology of devotion and surrender. (Prapatti). The basis for such an ideology, as Maharishi points out, lies in the life of the individual himself. The individual's life is both relative and absolute together. The individual is already in contact with the absolute Being. It is only the conscious contact that has to be established.

It has been previously explained, while dealing with Transcendental Meditation, that the practice does not require any thing on the part of the individual, except innocence and simplicity. The individual need not put forth any effort for that. "He must be devoid of any intellectual play or emotional twist", says Maharishi. (Page 95 — Science of Being and Art of Living—TM).

Such simplicity and innocence is already deeply ingrained in the nature of each individual. Transcendental Meditation affords a technique to surrender oneself to the almighty power of nature, and arrive at the absolute eternal field of divine intelligence. Maharishi says, "Having arrived at that plane, one begins to enjoy the almighty power of nature, quite automatically for great good to himself." (Page 95- Science of Being and Art of Living—TM).

When we speak that one naturally begins to enjoy the almighty power of nature, it should be understood that is takes place on that almighty level of nature only and not on the level of human understanding or human life.

Thus, we find that it is within the reach of every human being to live life on the level of cosmic law, where he will naturally be enjoying the almighty power of Mother Nature. But it is not possible for him to understand that almighty power, or the cosmic law, and its various components, intricacies, and complexities, because all of them, lie outside the domain of the relative field of human intellect and understanding. It is pointed out that the technique of how to make full use of the almighty power of nature cannot be, on the level of thinking, understanding, reasoning, discriminating or feeling. It is on the level of being only. Therefore the field of surrendering is never on the level of thinking; it is on the level of being only.

Many aspirants who practice the philosophy of surrender to God or Mother Nature (Prapatti) try to surrender on the level of thinking. They make a mood of surrender to God, and mood making necessarily is on the level of gross conscious thinking.

Maharishi observes, thinking, "I have surrendered to God", and making a mood of that surrender, does not carry the aspirant any far. It only creates dullness, and passivity on the part of the individual, and deprives him of the opportunity to advance in active life.

Maharishi's observation on the philosophy of surrender seems to be a break through and to be immensely helpful to the students of metaphysics. Here is, what he says, "True surrender to God cannot be on the thinking level. This sense of surrender is always on the level of Being, and, unless the level of Being is consciously gained by the mind, any attempt at making a mood of surrender will only result in a fanciful passivity of individual life and not a grand and successful attunement with the almighty power of nature". (Page 96 — Science of Being and Art of Living—TM).

We have previously seen that the conscious mind should transcend thinking and feeling, to arrive at the place of Being. Unless the conscious mind is infused with the state of divine Being, the state of surrender does not arise. As long as the individual remains on the thinking level, he maintains his identity and because to maintain a thought, be it a thought of surrender, one has to remain an individual thinker. "As long as the individuality is maintained, the state of surrender cannot be" says Maharishi. (Page 96 — Science of Being and Art of Living—TM).

Maharishi points out that surrender to the almighty will be God, surrender to the almighty nature (Prapatti), is the most advanced ideology of life. If one really surrenders, one loses the petty individuality of the time-space-causation-bound-mind, and gains the unlimited eternal status of transcendental consciousness, which is easily arrived at, by the system of Transcendental Meditation. Maharishi observes, that the words "Surrender to the will of god" are significant, which provide a direct way for the individual, to gain the almighty power. But for the past many centuries, without a technique of easily transcending the limits of relative existence being available, the above expression "Surrender to the will of God" has remained merely as an idea, and has had no practical significance for the life of the aspirants. It has come to mean an abstract, metaphysical or mystical sense of life. But with the knowledge of Transcendental Meditation, these words have become a significant, practical reality of life. They are no longer shrouded in the garb of mysticism. They now represent the truth of daily experience, and through this experience, comes the ability of making full use of the almighty power.

It is only the regular practice of Transcendental Meditation that brings a man to that status, where he finds himself placed in the situation, in which the almighty power of nature works for him. It is not, that he is required to make use of it, but that he is given the full advantage of it.

But without raising to a state of cosmic consciousness, or at least, putting oneself on the path, Maharishi observes, that it is simply not possible to make use of even the partial strength of Mother Nature, not to speak of the almighty power.

Maharishi describes in glowing terms the qualification which accrue to the person who has established within himself a state of natural attunement with cosmic Being.

He observes that the whole of nature moves in accordance with his needs; all his desires are in accordance with the cosmic purpose, and his life serves the purpose of cosmic evolution. He is in the hands of God, for the purpose of God, and God is for him and for his purpose. He uses the almighty power of Mother Nature, and Mother Nature uses his life, for the glorious purpose of creation and evolution, Maharishi concludes, "Very fortunate is he". Maharishi deprecates the use of the super natural powers of creation, by some, who contact the spirit world, through a medium, or through invoking spirits. He says, any acquisition of powers through such means, can be only on a very limited level of strength, because no spirit is in position of the total power of nature. There may be spirits who may be more powerful than man, but invoking these spirits, or behaving as a medium for them, is not a practice to be encouraged. Maharishi observed that in order to make people receive the right technique, to make full use of the almighty power of nature, it becomes necessary that large number of teachers of meditation, be available every where. This makes it possible for the life of all people to be set naturally on a sound footing, so as to enable them enjoy the great benefits of the almighty power of nature.

He speaks about other types of aspirants who with a view to develop higher powers take up to the practices of concentration and control of the mind. After years of practice, they seem to achieve something in line with their aspirations, but the gain that they have achieved is not commensurate with the great effort that they have put in over the years, even for a small achievement. This amounts to a waste of human aspirations, and time, and a waste of the great possibilities of achievements, on the way to higher power. We know that all the psychic powers belong to the field of Being. Therefore, if there could be a way, to directly come in contact and be familiar with the field of Being, then it is certain that all the psychic powers and all the powers of nature, belonging to almighty eternal Being will be available. So, when there is a chance, through the practice of Transcendental Meditation for every on to contact Being, in an easy manner, Maharishi observes, it is unwise to practice concentration or mind control, which is arduous and takes years to give appreciable results.

Thus, an open invitation is extended by Sri Maharishi, to all the seekers of power in the world, to rise and start the practice of Transcendental Meditation, and raise the standard of their consciousness to the plane of cosmic consciousness. By so doing, they gain the advantage of being naturally placed in a position, where the almighty power of Mother Nature will be at their disposal, and will naturally be serving the cause of their life.

This, Maharishi says, Mother Nature will do for them, without their intention, or, without their overtly trying to use the power of nature. He further says "All that they want or need, the need of their surroundings, and all concerned, will naturally be met in the most magnanimous and glorious ways". (Page 99 — Science of Being and Art of Living—TM).

Maharishi mentions about people who have been told to believe, that the power of positive thinking, is the greatest power of nature. They are advised to base their lives on positive thinking. Maharishi calls it childish, and ridiculous, to base one's life on the level of thinking.

Thinking can never be a profound stable basis of living, Being is the natural basis. He says one need not waste one's time in thinking positively, and waiting for the positive thought to be materialized. Instead, it is necessary for one to positively be. Positive Being, through the practice of Transcendental Meditation provides the greatest status to one's life. It brings him the possibility of the power of almighty nature in the day-do-day practical life. Thinking, on the other hand is imaginary. To make thinking, powerful, it is necessary to be. The technique of Being is the technique of making the thought powerful. Basing our life solely on positive thinking, will be basing our life, just, on an imaginary basis, which will be deprived of any stability factor. "Trying to attain the powers of nature on the basis of thinking is to delude oneself", says Maharishi. It is therefore, that the philosophy of positive thinking should be replaced by the philosophy of positive being. In man's life, it is not the science of mind that is the top most and most useful science of life. It is the science of Being that occupies the top most status in the sciences of life and living.

Maharishi therefore says, that the mind has to be supplemented by the power of Being. It is the power of Being which is the real basis of life, not the mind. All the material sciences, like physics, chemistry, biology, etc., pertain to the relative field of existence. Likewise, the field of mind is also a part of the relative field of existence. The science of mind, like any other science is merely the science of the relative fields of life. It is only the science of Being, that is the science of absolute eternal existence. It is the science of Being that could impart, a stable basis for life in the relative field of life.

It is the power of Being that must be aspired and acquired. It is easy for all people in the world to acquire it, even while they are engaged in the busy schedule of modern life.

The principle of making full use of the almighty power of nature, lies in the science of Being, which is realized by the regular practice of Transcendental Meditation.

Art of Being :

The Art of Being as defined by Maharishi implies that the value of Being should not be lost in the different spheres of life. Further, it should be naturally and fully retained in all spheres of life under all circumstances, in all the states of consciousness. It should glorify all aspects of life leading to fulfillment.

We have seen that the nature of Being is bliss consciousness of absolute nature and eternal status.

Art of Being, therefore involves that the concentrated state of happiness should be constantly lived under all circumstance. This would ensure that life will be blissful, naturally free from suffering, misery, tension, confusion and disharmony. The different aspects of life like thinking, speaking, acting and behaving, should become and remain permeated with the conscious awareness of being. Thereby, man lives a life with the full value of Being permeating all shapers of his life.

In practice, the art of being involves that man first finds Being in the innermost level of his life and brings it out from the transcendental field of unmanifested nature, into the relative existence. He first explores the region of being , by taking the conscious mind from the gross field of relative experience to the field of the unmanifested Being, and then brings the mind out, well infused with the value of being.

Hence the art of being, or the technique of gaining that state of being lies in contacting being and living it.

Transcendental Meditation is the practical technique for the art of Being. Let us now consider some of the different aspects of life which are enriched by the art of Being, or, the technique of gaining that state of being by Transcendental Meditation.

Art of Being on the level of thinking :

When being is maintained at the conscious level, all the thoughts naturally will be at the level of Being. Then thinking and Being find their co-existence this is the art of being in thinking.

So, when one thinks with the conscious mind established at the level of being, then, being is naturally maintained through the process of thinking. The art of Being with regard to thinking, therefore requires the infusion of the value of the transcendental being into the nature of the mind.

Maharishi analyses the relationship of thought with Being. Mind's essential nature is Being. The process of thinking brings the mind out of its essential nature, namely its Being. It is therefore clear that the process of thinking is opposed to the state of being. This is the reason why, the mind transcends the subtlest state of thinking, before it is able to arrive at the state of Being. When it starts thinking again, it must come out of the transcendental field of Being.

It is therefore, that the conscious mind is either engaged in the process of thinking, or, is in the transcendental state of pure being.

Thus, we see thinking is in a way of challenge to Being. This is only because, the mind ahs not been trained to hold being and the thought simultaneously. In general, the ingrained habit of the mind to remain mostly in the field of thinking, poses a challenge to the state of Being. With the practice of Transcendental Meditation, the conscious mind goes to the source of thought, and becomes familiar with the state of Being. On this aspect, Maharishi observes, "then the state of pure being is so harmonious, blissful, and so pure in its nature that the mind, having become familiar with it, will not part with it under any circumstances. It is then, that the nature of the mind is transformed into he very nature of Being, so that, the mind, while yet remaining a thinking mind, is naturally established in the field of Being. This is the art of Being in the field of thought". (Page 103, — Science of Being and Art of Living—TM).

If the mind is without being, the process of thinking is as though lifeless. If the mind is not familiar with Being the process of thinking and the thought force are very weak. This will result in weak activity and the resulting accomplishments are not satisfying and life's fulfillment is not achieved. So, it is the art of Being while thinking, that is the basis of all accomplishments and fulfillment in life. This is secured by the regular practice of Transcendental Meditation.

When we speak of the art of being on the level of thinking it means that the state of Being should be created in the mind. This can only happen by brining the attention of the mind to the transcendental field of Being. It cannot be accomplished by any other process.

Maharishi, here, makes an important distinction between thought and state. He observes, that any attempt to hold the awareness of being at the conscious level, without actually bringing the conscious mind to the field of transcendental being, through the practice of Transcendental Meditation, could only result in the conscious mind entertaining the thought of being only. When the conscious mind entertains the thought of being it is deprived, or devoid of the state of being, because, the thought of being is not the state of being itself. He further observes that, any attempt to hold the thought of Being, with the hope of maintaining the awareness of Being on the conscious level will only result in division of the mind. On this aspect Maharishi observes, "the practice of cherishing the thought of being will, neither cultivate being in the mind, nor, will it allow the full mind to be engaged in the thinking process. This means neither being nor the thinking will be profound. (Page 103,—Science of Being and Art of Living—TM).

Maharishi refers to some misguided schools of thought, which provoke the seekers of truth, to maintain awareness of being on the conscious level, while they are engaged in thinking speaking, or acting. He deprecates such attempts to maintain being, or try to maintain self awareness on the conscious being, or try to maintain self awareness on the conscious thinking level, without allowing the mind to transcend, as being merely futile attempts, to live being in life. They would only result in creating a false idea about the state of realization of being during thinking or activity.

He further emphasizes, that being is a state of life to be lived at the transcendental level. It cannot be thought and lived. It is naturally lived without a thought about it. He gives the reason why, the state of Being has gone out of our consciousness. It is because, that we have not been acquainted with the field of transcendental pure being. For that, the only way is, that the conscious attention should be brought from the gross state of thinking, to the subtlest state of thought and then transcending it, where the transcendental field of being is reached.

Therefore, the art of being with regard to the thinking lies in the technique of gaining the state of being, by contacting being and living it. It lies in the system of Transcendental Meditation.

The practice of Transcendental Meditation which maintains Being on the level of thinking, is also the practice of maintaining being on the level of speaking. The difference will be only in scale. Greater practice of Transcendental Meditation will be needed for maintaining being at the level of speaking.

Thus, the art of being at the level of speaking lies in the regular and steady practice of Transcendental Meditation. This helps to bring being to fullness on the level of the mind at all times, making it possible for thinking and speaking, to be in the same flow, thus introducing harmony in the life of the individual. It furthers the process of his evolution and also helps the process of cosmic evolution.

Breathing and Art of Being :

Maharishi explains breathing as follows :

It is breathing that lies between the individual being and cosmic being. It connects the individual life stream with the eternal cosmic ocean of life. It is breathing that sets forth an individual life stream out of the cosmic ocean of being.

In its subtlest aspect breathing is referred to, as prana. Prana is the vibratory nature of Being. It is prana that transforms the unmanifested ocean of being into the manifested life stream of individual beings (Jivas). The transcendental omnipresent absolute cosmic being, on account of its own nature prana, vibrates into manifested individual streams of life. Prana then, assumes the role of breathing which maintains the individual life stream, and keeps it connected at its basis with the cosmic life of the absolute.

At every rise of the breath, the cosmic prana gets the identity of the individual life force, and at every fall of the breath, the stream of individual life contacts cosmic being, so that, between the fall and rise of the breath, the state of the individual life is in communion with cosmic being. It is thus seen that breathing on the one hand, produces individual life from the cosmic life, and on the other, it maintains the harmony of the individual, in the tune with the cosmic being. The art of being with regard to breathing means, that , even while the breath is in action, the contact of the individual life stream with the eternal life of cosmic being is not broken.

It is first necessary to see, how the breathing starts, and what is it, that makes the breath, or prana, emerge from being. We have seen that prana is the vibratory nature of being. Maharishi examines the question, how, and why, the vibratory nature of being chooses a particular pattern giving rise to a specific steam of the individual life by virtue of breathing. Breathing as we have seen, sets forth the steam of the individual life.

It looks certain, that there should be something more than mere prana, which brings forth the life of a particular individual. What is there, other than prana, which is responsible for the set pattern of breathing?

Maharishi examines this question by taking the example of the tree to illustrate the phenomenon. In the case of the tree it is the sap which is its essential constituent. The whole tree consisting of the trunk, leaves, flowers and fruits is nothing but the expression of this nourishment. The sap is received by the whole tree from the area surrounding the tree in a natural process of evolution. But, it can be seen, that any amount of sap present in the earth, will not be able to produce the specific pattern of the tree, unless the seed of the tree is available. It is therefore, the seed of the tree that determines the specific pattern of the tree. Without the seed the sap has no basis to express itself.

In the above example, we can consider the sap to be transcendental being of the absolute cosmic life, and the three as the individual stream of life. Being is eternally present there, but, to have a specific pattern of individual life, being needs the seed of that pattern. Without a specific seed, no specific individual life could manifest out of unmanifested omnipresent being. What is this seed of the individual life through which the omnipresent being, by its own nature prana, manifests into an individual life stream?

Maharishi explains this aspect further. The seed of individual life, is just like the seed of a tree which is nothing but the sap in its most highly evolved state of expression. The sap passing through all the cycles of evolution, reaches its highest state of evolution in a fully grown tree and appears as a seed. Thus the seed therefore signifies the most highly developed state of the tree, and it is the most highly concentrated state of the sap. Then, that seed, becomes the cause of attracting the sap and growing into a tree again.

Being, on account of its vibratory nature, expresses itself as prana, on which will be based the sprouting of a thought, which in turn develops into a desire which leads to action, and when the action is completed, the fruit of action marks the full growth of the tree of thought, or desire. When the fruit of action is experienced, there will be an impression of the experience and this impression will be like the concentrated state of a seed, which is capable of giving rise to future desires and action. Thus, it is found that the case of the cycle of seed and tree, is like the case of the cycle of thought, desire, action fruit of action, and its impression. Here the seed is like a thought, and the soil from which the sap is drawn for the nourishment of the seed, is being, which lies at the basis of thought.

One the coming in to the world, of the individual life of sat pattern, Maharishi, has this to say.

The seed of individual life is nothing, but the expression of unmanifested Being, in the most highly evolved state of manifestation. Omnipresent being of unmanifested nature, first manifests as a thought. It goes through all the cycles of evolution, and reaches the climax of the evolution of the thought, in the fruit of the action.

The impression of the experience of the fruit of action, becomes the seed for future thought. By virtue of the seed-thought, being, begins to express itself in the stream of an individual life of set pattern.

Thus we see being, expressing itself in different degrees of manifestation and passing though the different cycles of evolution and arriving at a point, where it is capable of being the seed for the future of the individual.

We have seen previously that prana is the vibratory nature of being. Unmanifested being does not need the help of any outside instrumentality, to cause it to vibrate. It does so by its own nature. The true nature of being is that it not only maintains its status of eternal absolute being, while vibrating, but also maintains the transitory levels of life, life after life, in the ever changing aspects of manifested relative existence.

So, when prana manifests, being vibrates and by vibrating, it assumes the role of a particular pattern of breathing or life stream, in accordance with the individual life.

Maharishi speaking on these aspects observes, "the individual seed of life, is the unfulfilled karma of the past life of man. The sum total of all the unfulfilled desires is the seed of the individual that molds vibrating being, into a specific life stream of an individual. So, the prana in conjunction with the desire forms the mind. And prana devoid of its association with the mind forms matter. This is how the subjective and objective aspects of the individual life come into existence." (Page 108, — Science of Being and Art of Living—TM).

From the above, it is clear that in essence it is being that expresses. In the life of the tree, it is the sap which expresses itself in different aspects of the tree. In a similar manner. It is being, which expresses itself as different aspects of the individual. Just as, in the case of a tree, it is the seed which shapes the pattern of the sap into a tree, in an individual life, it is the impression (samskara) of the experience of the past life, that shape being into a specific pattern of individual life force, or prana.

Thus it is found that prana, or its gross aspect, breathing is the fundamental aspect of the life stream of the individual. It is the link between the individual life stream and the oceans of cosmic life energy. It is by virtue of mind, in conjunction with prana, that the whole stream of individual life is set into a specific pattern.

The art of being with regard to breathing, lies in the maintenance of the value of being in the nature of the mind, because, breath in, is the result of the combination of prana and mind, and prana and mind are not absolutely two different thing.

It is seen that mind includes within its role, the feature of prana, without prana, there could not be mind, and without the mind, prana is just the nature of being, something of absolute value, beyond the relative life. Therefore, in order to maintain being on the level of breathing, it is primarily necessary, to bring being into the level of the mind.

With the practice of Transcendental Meditation, when the mind becomes saturated with Being, breathing is on the level of Being. Maharishi says with respect to this state, "Breathing is found in harmony, with the rhythm of nature, and the individual life whose breathing has been transformed on the level of being, breaths in the harmony and rhythm of cosmic life. The breathing then gains the subtle state of vibrating prana". (Page 109, — Science of Being and Art of Living—TM).

The breathing of individual is thus, the nature of cosmic being, the breathing of the individual then, is the vibrating prana, says Maharishi. Thus the art of being and breathing, is the art of raising the status of the individual to the state of eternal cosmic Being.

The fulfillment of this art, is found in the regular practice of Transcendental Meditation.

Art of Being, on the level of experience :

In the case of an experience, the object coming in contract with the senses of experience, leaves an impression of the object on the mind of the experiencer and the essential nature of the mind is overshadowed. It is thus seen, that the process of experience is a process which throws being out of sight. This is termed identification. It is as though, the subject within becomes identified with the object outside, and loses its essential nature, its being. Thus it is found that an experience brings the experiencer out of his own being.

The art of being on the level of experience means, that during the experience of an object, there should be no overthrowing of the status of being from the mind. It means that the mind should be able to maintain being, while experiencing the object.

We have seen previously, that by the regular practice of Transcendental Meditation, being begins to be maintained at the level of experience or perception, and the mind maintains its essential nature namely its being, even while it experiences the object. Thereby the experiencer remains unbound by the impact of the experience. Further, the experiencer lives in the complete freedom of fullness of being, and at the same time experiences the outside world around him.

Maharishi further says, that in a state where being is full maintained in the nature of the mind, the process of experience becomes powerful.

This art of being on the level of experience, is the skill of fully integrated life, where one is able to live all the values of the transcendental absolute bliss consciousness of being, along with the experience of various aspects of the relative creation of material and physical values. The life of the individual will then be, in an integrated state with cosmic life. Thereby the individual life finds its fulfillment.

Without the art of being on the level of experience, the process of experience makes the subject so fully identified with the object that the impression of the value of the object becomes very strong in the mind. This impression, according to Maharishi is held fast in the mind, as a seed for future desire for the same experience. This is how the cycle of experience, impression, desire-experience, impression, desire continues to be, and the cycle of birth and death goes on.

It should be understood that the cause of rebirth is the unfulfilled desires of past life. If a person wants to accomplish something in this life, but fails to do so before the body ceases to function, he dies without the fulfillment of his desire. Because of this unfulfillment, the inner man (mind) goes to create another body though which the unfulfilled desires of previous life may be fulfilled. So it happens, that one's own desire is the cause of rebirth. Man is born in this life, with the impressions (Samskaras or Vasanas) of the experiences of past life, which have laid down deep impression of their values. These impressions become the seed for future desires, and this cycle of experience, impression, desire takes man from birth to birth, and the cycle of birth and death continues, until this cycle of experience and impression is broken.

If being is maintained at the level of experience, it will not allow any deep impression of the object on the mind; in that case the impression will be just enough, to give the experience of the object, to allow the perception to be. It will not allow anything deeper. Because the mind is full of the value of being, and being in its nature is bliss consciousness, the impressions of the experience of the transitory nature of the objects in the relative field naturally fail to make a great impression on the mind. Being so, Maharishi says, that this impression is not deep enough to work as a seed for future action. To make the point clear, he gives the example of the tongue saturated with the taste of saccharin failing to register the impression of other varieties of sweetmeat, because the joy of the sweetmeat is not as great as the sweetness of the saccharin. Similarly the mind, having been full with the bliss of being, feels so contented that, although it experiences the object, the value of the object fails to register a deep impression on the mind. When being is maintained at the level of experience, then, the impression of the object on the mind is not very deep. Maharishi compares this impression to the impression of a line drawn on water, which is drawn but, simultaneously erased. In a like manner the impression of the object on the mind full with being, is just enough to give the experience of the object. On the other hand, the impression of the object on the mind, without the value of being, is compared to the impression of a line drawn on stone, difficult to erase.

A mind devoid of the value of being, is always under the bondage of experience. This gives rise to the cycle of impression, desire and action. It is only the technique of Transcendental Meditation, that establishes being in the mind, and naturally allows it to live the value of being, along with the values of the outer experiences.

Thus we find that the art of being on the level of experience is fulfilled, in the regular and steady practice of Transcendental Meditation/

Art of Being at the level of Behaviour :

We have already said that the mind established on the level of being behaves in conformity with the cosmic law and all the laws of nature.

The behaviour of one who meditates is very natural with other people, because, being naturally creeps into the nature of the mind.

It is important to note, that it is unstrained natural behaviour alone, that will help being to grow in the field of activity. Any unnatural manner of behaviour only strains the mind, but when one behaves innocently and naturally on all levels, the stream of life flows smoothly and in accord with the laws of nature.

Maharishi cautions against, man planning how to behave. He says, if a man plans how to behave, then the behaviour ceases to be natural. It is then no longer in conformity with the laws of nature. So, when it is said that the art of being on the level of behaviour lies in the regular practice of Transcendental Meditation, it should be added that, along with the practice, the aspirant should be very natural and innocent in his behaviour with others. Maharishi further emphasizes that it is not necessary that he should think much about how to behave, what to do, how to speak, or how to handle a situation. Let him wait for the situation to come, and then, let him handle it innocently and naturally. If the practice of Transcendental Meditation is regular and sustained, all behaviour on all levels will naturally be rewarding.

The art of Being on the level of behavour finds its fulfillment in the regular practice of Transcendental Meditation along with the very natural, innocent and easy manner of behavour and activity in the outside world.

Health and the Art of Being :

Maharishi defines health as Being. Good health is the state of Being, and evolving at the same time. Ill health brings disharmony in the state of Being and in the evolutionary process as well.

Maharishi attributes all suffering in life to not finding a way to establish being on the conscious level of life, thereby not eliminating discord, disharmony, dissension and disunity. If a way could be found to establish being on the conscious level, then perfect health would prevail on all levels of life.

It is previously stated that the all pervading eternal existence of being is the basis of all that exists in the universe and all that lives. It is the basis of the body, mind, and surroundings of the individual. The sap is the basis of all the branches, trunk, leaves and fruit of the tree, and when the sap fails to reach the surface levels of the tree, the outer aspects of the tree begin to suffer and wither away. In a similar manner, if being is not brought out to the conscious surface level of life, the outer aspects of life begin to suffer.

Therefore, if health and harmony are to be enjoyed in life, some how, the transcendental value of being must be brought out and infused into all aspects of life—body, mind, and surroundings, and a healthy co-ordination established between them.

Maharishi then examines, how the value of being could be brought out to the surface level of the mind, body and surroundings, it is this way the purpose of health would be served.

The art of brining Being to the level of the mind :

This means, that the value of the eternal being is maintained on the level of the mind under all circumstances, when the mind is engaged in thining, or experiencing, and when it is in the three states of consciousness of waking, dreaming, or deep sleep. Even when the mind is thinking or experiencing, the thought or the experience should not overshadows the essential nature of the mind, namely its being. When being is maintained on the level of the mind, the flow of the mind in thinking, or experiencing is in accordance with the laws of nature. It is then, that the individual is placed in the natural stream of evolution, and his thoughts are forceful and his experience is complete and deep. In such a situation both the individual and the universe gain.

To maintain being on the level of the mind, during the activities of the day, it is first necessary for the conscious mind to get itself acquainted with the state of being. We know that the state of being is of transcendental nature, and it is transcendental absolute consciousness. We have seen previously that, by the practice of Transcendental Meditation, the conscious mind is made to explore the deeper and the subtler levels of thought, until it reaches the subtlest thought and then transcending it, arrives at the state of transcendental being. In this way the conscious mind reaches transcendental being and becomes acquainted with it.

Transcendental Meditation is therefore the art of bringing the conscious mind, to the level of the transcendental being or bringing being within the range of the conscious mind. With continued and regular practice of Transcendental Meditation, the mind becomes more and more familiar with being, and eventually becomes rooted in its very nature. At this stage, even when the mind returns to the relative field to engage itself with the outside worldly activities, being remains permanent on the level of the conscious mind. This is how Transcendental Meditation maintains being on the level of the mind.

This technique of brining transcendental being to the level of the mind secures the following advantages :

1.   It enlarges the conscious capacity of the mind and enables the full mind to function.
2.   It brings to action the full potentialities of the mind.
3.   Nothing in the mind remains hidden, nothing remains sub-conscious, and everything becomes conscious. This makes every thought a very powerful thought.
4.   When the mind comes to the field of transcendental being, it is naturally set in harmony with all the laws of nature and in tune with the process of cosmic evolution.

Maharishi lists the further advantages of brining transcendental being to the level of the mind as below :

1.   Since the nature of being is absolute bliss consciousness, the mind becomes full with bliss consciousness and everlasting happiness comes to the conscious level of the mind.
2.   Since transcendental being is eternal and permanent, imperishable and unchanging, the very nature of the mind gets itself infused by this imperishable, eternal and unchanging aspect of being.

Speaking about this aspect, Maharishi observes, "Such a mind is stable, unwavering, steady and one pointed, while it is also blissful, contented, self contained and sharp". (Page 115, — Science of Being and Art of Living—TM).

It has been previously pointed out that transcendental absolute being is the source of all thought and of all creation. When the conscious mind is taken to that level in Transcendental Meditation, it comes in contact with the unlimited creative intelligence of absolute being. Great creative intelligence enters into the nature of the mind, and the mind gets the qualities of constructive imagination. The power of creative thinking increases and the mind gets the qualities of joyfulness and contentment.

Maharishi observes that the mind in tune with the field of being, gains the source of unlimited energy. Out of such a powerful and energetic mind, naturally powerful thoughts arise. It is also contended by Sri maharishi that every thought arising out of such a mind stimulates the nervous systems with great vitality and vigour and the nervous systems is thereby put to sustained and powerful activity. The body is thereby stimulated with such great force and fixity of purpose, that the thought is materialized and becomes a positive reality, achieving great success in the outside world without any delay or strain. The chance for the material realization of a thought becomes so great that the action becomes automatically forceful. This is said to be the result of brining transcendental being to the level of the mind its effect. On the individual in his day-to-day practical life.

Sri Maharishi cities another great advantage of being coming to the level of the mind. Even though the mind experiences the thought and action and all that goes with it in the relatives field of worldly activities, nothing is able to dislodge or overshadow being which has taken deep root in the very nature of the mind. This enables the mind to behave freely in thought and action in the perishable and ever changing activities of worldly life, and yet, remain firmly established in the eternal and imperishable nature of absolute being. Such a state is said to be a state of eternal freedom in life.

The art of being lies in the practice of Transcendental Meditation, which readily brings the mind out of the thinking process to the field of being, and brings being out of the transcendental, into the field of activity.

Maharishi emphasizes here, that the whole process of meditation involves experiencing subtle states of thinking, and thinking primarily depends upon the physical state of the nervous system. Therefore any factor which influences the physical condition of the nervous system, indirectly influences the process of meditation. It is seen that the physical state of the nervous system is maintained by the process of eating, drinking and breathing, and the factors of activity and rest, also have an influence. If all these factors are properly adjusted, so as to maintain the ideal physical state of the nervous system, then, the practice of Transcendental Meditation will be ideally successful. Eating improper food, and breathing of improper air. Will create dullness in the nervous system, and if in addition, one engages himself in activities subjecting the nervous system to fatigue and tension, then naturally, the mind will not be able to fathom the deeper levels of the thought process, and meditation itself will become less effective, and infusion of being into the nature of the mind will be unduly delayed. Therefore, it is highly important that proper care be taken in the selection of the type of food, drink and air. Maharishi says, that is has been found out by study, that wrong eating, and drinking of alcoholic beverages, is very detrimental to the overall well-being of a person. He observes that one should aim towards rectification of improper dietary habits.

Influence of Food :

Food is said to have great influence on the mind, because, what we eat and drink, makes the blood which sustains the nervous system. Therefore the quality of food affects greatly the quality of mind.

It is also important, apart from the quality of material in the food, how the food has been earned. Food earned by righteous means has a good influence on the mind. For example, if a man earns his living by theft, or other illegal, or unrighteous means, the quality of the food that is bought from that earning, produces those qualities in the mind. Further the tendencies of the mind, or the quality of the thoughts at the time of eating the food affect the mind and influence its quality. Maharishi, therefore recommends that a man should be either silent in pure thought, or have a good conversation with those at the table. He says, it is best to say a prayer before we begin to sat.

Influence of Activity :

The nervous system is also affected by the factor of activity and inactivity. Over activity makes it dull, and so does, lack of activity. A balance of activity and inactivity is necessary for maintaining the nervous system in a state of alertness, which is highly necessary for the success of the art of being on the level of the mind. If the body is fatigued, the nervous systems becomes dull and the mind beings to be drowsy, losing all capacity of experience. In such a state, the ability to experience the subtle states of thinking is not possible. There will, consequently, be no chance of success in meditation.

It is said that the state of being is the most normal and self-contained state of mind. Maharishi further says, that, when the mind is all in itself, it is the state of being. We have seen previously that the state of being consists, in brining the conscious mind to the subtlest state of thought, and transcending it to arrive at the state of self consciousness, or the state of pure being. In this state, the mind is left all by itself, without the experience of any object, and yet, it should not lose its ability of experience as it does in deep sleep.

To give rise to this state of being, the nervous systems has to be in a particular state of activity. In the particular state to give rise to the state of being, the nervous systems has to be suspended in such a way, that it is neither subjected to activity, nor, is it allowed to be non-active. This will be the state of being.

We shall now study how the nervous system functions, when the nervous systems is functioning, it gives rise to the experience of the object thought the senses of perception, and it engages itself in activity through the organs of action. Functioning in this manner, when it becomes fatigues, it reaches a condition in which it fails to perceive the world around it. If the fatigued is greater there will be no perception and the mind fails to experience. From this it is clear that the state of mind depends upon the physical condition of the nervous system, and we find that fatigue controls the state of experience. Hence it can be concluded, that, if the nervous system is passive with fatigue, there is no possibility of arriving at the state of being, and if the nervous systems is active, then also, it is not possible for the mind to gain the state of being.

Hence the factor of fatigue becomes an important factor to be considered in the art of being. The art of being therefore lies also in not subjecting the nervous system to great fatigue. It is therefore necessary, that the activity during the day should be such, that it does not leave the body tired, or the nervous systems fatigued. If the body is tired, the nervous system is put to tension and fatigue, and that state of suspension of the nervous system between activity and no activity will not be cultivated. Hence the pure state of being will not occur.

In addition to excessive activity, wrong eating and drinking also cause a great amount of dullness in the nervous system. This too is not conducive to the state of being.

Art of being, or bringing being to the level of the mind lies basically in the system of Transcendental Meditation. Transcendental

Meditation in turn is highly dependent on the state of the nervous system. It is therefore advisable, Maharishi says, that one should have regular habits of proper dies and activity. One should neither exert oneself excessively, nor one should remain inactive.

The practice of Transcendental Meditation, brings the mind to the field of transcendental being and infuses the conscious mind with an unlimited source of energy and thereby, helps the field of activity to be normal.

But one has to be cautions not to overspend the increase energy due to meditation, or otherwise, it may produce strain and fatigue to the nervous system hampering the effectiveness of meditation. Therefore, the art of being basically depends upon the habits of activity and rest.

It is pointed out by Maharishi that unregulated habits of diet, activity and rest are the result of an unbalanced state of mind. To bring the nervous system to the right condition of rest, activity and nourishment, it is essential that a balanced state of mind be cultivated. The mind will be balanced only when it has a chance of being contented due to the experience of great happiness. It is only the experience of bliss consciousness that can create a balanced mind, and this is automatically achieved through the system of Transcendental Meditation.

Thus, we find that the art of being on the level of the mind finds its fulfillment in the regular practice of Transcendental Meditation, and its success depends upon maintaining a regulated life consisting of regular habits and proper way of life.

The art of being on the level of senses :

There are five senses of perception and five organs of action. The five senses of perception are, sight, smell, hearing, taste and tough. The five organs of action are the hands, feet, tongue and the two organs of elimination. The mind perceives thought the five senses and acts through the five organs of action. For perception the mind contacts the external world, through the senses, and for action, the mind is brought to bear upon the external world through the organs of action.

The art of being on the level of senses is said to exist when the senses and organs, retain being under all circumstances.

Maharishi describes the art of being with regard to senses thus. The art of being, with regard to the senses means that they experience the object while they remain saturated with the essential nature of being-bliss of being. This would result in the object being thoroughly perceived, but the object fails to overpower the senses to the extent that they become slaves to the object.

Maharishi gives the example of saccharin and says, that, with the intense sweetness of saccharin on the tongue, the taste of other sweets fails to make an impression. Similarly, when the senses are saturated with the bliss of being, the small transitory joys of objects fail to bind the senses and do not make a lasting impression on them.

When being is on the level of the senses the senses receive their full contentment in bliss consciousness. They would then, experience the variety of joys of the objects in the relative world, without in any way being bound by them, because, they are bound in the eternal value of the unlimited bliss of the absolute.

In such a state of contentment in bliss consciousness, the senses do not entice the mind to wander in search of greater happiness. This is because, the bliss of being is already permeating the level of the senses, through the mind's saturation with being, and there is nothing for the senses to lure the mind in search of greater happiness.

In such a state of contentment of the senses, when the senses experience the outside objects, the result of the experience is completely harmonious with the surroundings, and for the body and mind of the individual as well.

Maharishi says regarding such a state of perception, "when the eyes see a beautiful scene, the sight is pure, the vision is full; one is free from any malice or sinful perception. All is right on the level of perception, all is virtuous, moral and is in the natural stream of evolution". (Page 121, — Science of Being and Art of Living—TM).

Maharishi further averse that permeation of the level of the senses by the bliss of transcendental being is very necessary for keeping the senses in a state of contentment. The nature of the senses is such, that they want to enjoy more. This, he says, is a legitimate desire. It is only by brining the bliss of transcendental being on to the level of the senses, that they become established in that level of contentment, which is unshakable and irresistible. It is only by thus remaining in contentment, they remain in freedom from the bondage of the impressions of their experiences. This is the result of the practice of the art of being on the level of the senses.

It is achieved by the regular practice of the system of Transcendental Meditation, which brings out a state of infusion of the value of being on the level of the senses.

Maharishi, then deals with the mechanics of Transcendental Meditation, which brings out a state of infusion of the value of being on the level of the senses is achieved.

It is necessary that we should know the full range of the senses. Ordinarily when we see, our eyes are open, and the mind associates itself with the open eye and comes in contact with the object facing it. This is how perception occurs. But it is also our experience, that the sense of sight is not merely limited to seeing with the open eyes. Even with closed eyes, it is possible to perceive an object with the mind. This mental perception or cognition of an object with the closed eyes will also be by means of the sense of sight. This makes it clear, that the sense of sight ranges in its ability to cognise from the gross level of perception to the subtle.

It can therefore be said, that the mind associating itself with the gross level of the senses perceives the corresponding gross level of the object; the mind associating itself with the subtle level of the senses perceives the corresponding subtle level of the object, and when the mind is carried to the subtlest level of the object, the mind associating itself with the subtlest level of the senses, perceives the corresponding subtlest level of the object.

Hence, the open eyes correspond to the gross level of the sense of sight only. In a similar manner, when a sound can be heard or becomes audible, it is the perception of the gross sound, as a result of the mind associating itself with the gross level of the sense of hearing.

When one speaks within oneself and the sound is not audible, only the mind hears the sound because the mind associates itself with the subtle level of the sense of hearing. During Transcendental Meditation, it is found that the mind perceives very refined state of thought. It is because, the mind associates itself with the very subtle state of the sense of hearing. Thus we find, that during meditation the finest ability of the sense of perception is brought to play, whereas Ordinarily, in our daily life, we continue to use only the gross level of the senses.

When the mind makes use of the finest level of the senses, the entire range of the senses becomes alive. During Transcendental Meditation, on the way to transcending, the mind makes alive the entire range of the field of the senses through which Transcendental Meditation is carried on.

Maharishi points out "when the full range of the whole field of the senses is made alive, being comes to the level of the senses." (Page 122,— Science of Being and Art of Living—TM).

With the full range of the whole field of the senses being made alive, the resulting increase in strength and power of the senses is capable of gaining the highest level of happiness. But, when only a small portion of the senses is utilized for the experience of the objective world, the faculty of the sense of experience is not fully used and in such a state, it is natural for the senses to be fascinated by the small joy of the object in the world.

It is also seen, that in the gross level of creation the contact of the sense and object does not produce great joy. The degree of joy increases as the sense begins to appreciate the subtler levels of creation. During Transcendental Meditation the organ of speech (sense of hearing) experiences subtler levels of thought. The charm increases at every subtler level of experience. As the charm increases the organ becomes more and more capable of experiencing increased happiness and ultimately, when the direct perception of the subtlest state occurs, the organ will have become capable of experiencing the highest degree of happiness in the relative field.

When the mind transcends that happiness and goes beyond the realm of sensory perception, the bliss of the Absolute becomes a direct experience. Then the mind completely becomes it. When the mind, fully saturated with being, comes back into the field of objective experience, the sense which had through the process of meditation tasted the greatest degree of happiness in the relative field, become saturated with the bliss of being and remains contents. This is how, the transcendental bliss of being comes to the level of the senses.

Therefore, the art of brining the level of being is also the art of brining eternal contentment to the level of the senses and this is fulfilled by the art of Transcendental Meditation.

Just as the mind is like an ocean of great depth, the field of the senses also has great depth. With meditation, the mind begins to make the deepest level of the senses active.

This system of Transcendental Meditation, is a way to bring the level of being into the level of the senses. It enables the senses to work with their full capacity while at the same time, to be free from the binding influence of experience. This is the art of Being on the level of the senses.

The body and the art of Being :

Maharishi describes the body as the end organ, or the external expression of the nervous system. Transcendental Meditation must secure that the body functions to its fullest capacity without losing the level of being.

Through the practice of Transcendental Meditation a state of nervous system is created such that, the entire nervous system is brought, to a level of no activity and no passivity, to a state of restful alertness. This is said to be its most healthy state as we shall see later. By bringing the nervous system to this level between activity and no activity, Being comes to the level of the body. This is the art of being with regard to the body. Speaking about this, Maharishi says, "The entire nervous system and the body rise to that state of suspension, which knows no change and allows the body to exist in the fullness of life". (Page 124, — Science of Being and Art of Living—TM).

Maharishi further points out, that people who are practicing the system of Transcendental Meditation are naturally allowing their nervous system to be conditioned in the above, laudable state. He invites experimental physiologists to discover the details of the physiology of an evolving man, by conducting experimentation with the subjects of Transcendental Meditation. Who are available everywhere in the world.

Through the art of Being, with regard to the body, the body is maintained to last longer, to be energetic and lively, to be free from diseases, and its different parts to function in good co-ordination with one another. Further, the body's co-ordination with the mind through the nervous systems is always strong, and its relationship with the outside surroundings is firm and useful to both the body and the surroundings.

To secure such a condition it is necessary to bring the mind to the level of being, so that, the nervous system along with its end organ, the body, is simultaneously established on the level of being. Through the system of Transcendental Meditation, the body is brought to a state of activity and no activity the level of being. Therefore, the art of being with regard to the body finds its fulfillment in the regular practice of Transcendental Meditation.

The nervous System and art of Being :

The art of being with regard to the nervous, system means that the nervous system should function to its fullest capacity under all conditions without losing being

It is seen that for any experience to be possible, it is required that the nervous system should set itself in a particular state of condition. Experience in any state of consciousness—waking, dreaming, or sleeping—is rendered possible only by a corresponding set up of a particular state of the nervous system. The vision of an object is made possible only by the nervous system setting itself in a specific condition, which makes it possible for the eyes to remain open, and for the image of the object to enter upon the retina of the eye, and the particular impulses to be carried to the cortex. If the nervous system does not set itself in this specific manner, then the experience of the object does not take place. Therefore, for any experience to occur, the specific set up of the nervous system is necessary. This is true for all experiences.

The art of being with respect of the nervous system means that the nervous system, whether it is subjected to the conditions of the wakeful, dreaming, or deep-sleep states, should never lose that state which it gains during the experience of the transcendental Being. This is the art of being with regard to the nervous system.

It seems at first sight that this retention of the state of transcendental being is impossible, because, experience has it, that the nervous system cannot be subjected to two different conditions simultaneously, so as to have two different states of consciousness to be experienced. The nervous system can only be conditioned to one state at a time, either wakeful, dreaming, deep sleep, or transcendental.

Maharishi at this stage, makes an important contribution of far reaching importance to modern metaphysical thought. He says, "But a close scrutiny will reveal that it is within the capacity of man, to subject that nervous system to a state which will for all time maintain the level of Being, as the very basis of all the conditions responsible for giving rise to the experiences of any of these states— wakeful, dreaming, or deep sleep. The human nervous system is the most complete in the Almighty's creation". (Page 124,—Science of Being and Art of Living—TM).

Maharishi thus furnishes a sure and a permanent basis for the maintenance of the level of being in the physiological set-up of man, and thereby brings being, on to the level of the human nervous system, to be maintained in a permanent manner as a basis for all the experiences of man in the relative field of existence.

The Art of Being with respect to the nervous system is therefore the skill which accomplishes such a permanent state of the nervous systems, which while maintaining the level of being, allows the experiences of waking, dreaming, and deep sleep states to occur.

We shall next examine how these states occur in practice. Maharishi explains the different phenomena thus.

The experience in the wakeful state occurs when the mind is brought to bear on the outside world through the machinery of the nervous system. The nervous system activates the senses and the body, brings the mind in contact with the outside world, and produces the specific experience. On account of sustained activity like this, when the senses and the entire nervous system connected with them become fatigued, the mind loses contact with the sense and the outside world. This brings to an end the experiences of the wakeful state. As long as the mind is discontented it continues to be active. But the nervous system on the level of the senses being tired, the mind fails to experience the outside world of the wakeful experiences. On account of the mind's discontentment and continued desire to be active, some other parts of the nervous system receive the mind's commands. The other part of the nervous system which receives the command then becomes active, and stimulates the subtler regions of the senses, which are not commonly used for the experiences of the wakeful state. This gives rise to the illusionary experiences of the dream state. When the subtler regions oft the senses and the nervous system function o the illusionary level for sometime, the subtler regions of the nervous system become tired and the ability of perception of the illusionary experiences is lost giving rise to a state of no experience, that of deep sleep.

During Transcendental Meditation however, the nervous system is naturally subjected to a condition, different from the conditions, which give rise to the experiences of wakeful dreaming, or deep sleep states. In this condition during Transcendental Meditation, the nervous system gains a condition capable of giving rise to the experience of pure being. This experience of pure being is said to be the experience of transcendental consciousness.

In the states of waking, dreaming, or deep sleep, the nervous system is found to be commonly fluctuating only between the conditions of wakefulness, dreaming, and deep sleep. But through the practice of Transcendental Meditation it reaches a new status. Sri Maharishi argues, that this status could be located at the junction of any two of the three states of consciousness—wakeful, dreaming and deep sleep. And at this point of junction, he says lies the hope for attaining the art of being on the level of the nervous system.

Maharishi further points out that it is possible to maintain the state of the nervous system necessary for maintaining the state of being a permanent way, while allowing at the same time, the activity or inactivity in certain parts of the nervous system, to give rise to the experience of the usual states of waking, dreaming and sleeping, one after the other.

Maharishi adduces certain reasons in support of the existence simultaneously, of the different types of conditioning of the nervous system.

The reasons adduced by him are :

1. The state of the nervous system which gives rise to the experience of the transcendental being is a state unlike those giving rise to the experiences of waking, dreaming or sleeping states.

2. The state of the nervous system giving rise to the experience of being is located between any two of the three states, waking, dreaming or deep sleep.

3. It is a state, where the entire nervous system is suspended between activity and inactivity.

4. In none of the three states of waking, dreaming or deep sleep is the entire nervous system subjected to one type of conditioning.

5.   It is therefore possible to maintain the state of the nervous
      system necessary for the state of being in a permanent
      way.

Under Transcendental Meditation, we have seen that, by following
the thought into its subtle states, and transcending the subtlest state,
the conscious mind arrives at the transcendental consciousness.
This explains that the state of transcendental being, is located as
pure consciousness between the rising of two thoughts. It can be
seen that at the end of the subtlest aspect of the wakeful state, prior
to the beginning of the subtlest aspect of the dream state, lies the
transcendental state of pure being, or between the consciousness of
the wakeful state, and that of the dreaming state, lies the state of
pure consciousness.

This is the art of being, with regard to the nervous system, which
establishes a permanent state of the nervous system—the state
which maintains the level of being, and yet, allows the experiences
to occur under the conditions of the wakeful dreaming or deep—
sleep states.

The surroundings and the art of Being :

The art of being with regard to the surroundings means, that
being maintains itself whatever the surroundings, or circumstances.
This means, fullness of life is maintained irrespective of the
surroundings, whether the surroundings are good or bad, favourable
or unfavourable, harmful or useful virtuous or sinful. Under all
circumstances being maintains the fullness of life, of intelligence,
love, joyfulness and energy in the surroundings. This results in the
improvement of surroundings in everyway. It makes the surroundings
useful for the individual for the purpose of cosmic evolution and for
the universe.

If the individual maintains his being under all circumstances and
in all surroundings, his actions definitely improve the surroundings,
if they need improvement. Because the individual is established in
being, he will be radiating great contentment, great intelligence and
creativity.

KARMA and the Art of Being or action at the level of Being :

Maharishi's views on karma are summarized below:

The philosophy of karma according to Maharishi, is a simple philosophy of action and reaction. Karma has its varied meaning according to the context. It may mean action, force of action fruit of action, or impression of the experience or action. The word karma itself has no significance of good or bad; it simply pertains to action or activity. Good karma signifies good action, and bad karma means bad action, but karma itself means action. Maharishi explains that the law of conservation of energy supports the theory of karma. Every action that one performs has its results or reaction for the doer and surroundings.

Maharishi gives the example of a stone thrown into a pond to illustrate the effect of karma. If you throw a stone into a pond and produce an action, the stone sinks but it produces waves. They travel far and wide, until they each the shore and strike and produce their effect on the sand particles. The influence of the waves is felt everywhere allover the pond and shore. Similarly any action of an individual produces reaction, influence or effects in the doer and in the surroundings. Every thought, word and action of an individual produces waves of influence in the surrounding atmosphere. The quality of the influence depends upon the quality of the action. The degree of reaction spread in the surroundings, depends upon the strength of action.

Thus we find that we are every moment of our lives, producing waves of influence in the atmosphere by the breathing, thinking, speaking and our acting and behaving in the world. Just as in the case of a pond the influence of a wave spreads over the whole of the pond however small it may be, so also, the vibrations set forth by an action travel around the doer striking against each and everything, traveling far and wide and striking everything in the surroundings.

They strike against everything on the earth, on the moon, the sun and the stars, and keep on traveling in the entire field of the universe, influencing everything that they come across. The influence may be very small and negligible, but it does exist. The reaction created by the striking of these vibrations travel back and influence the doer, just as a rubber ball thrown against a wall is bounced back. The influence depends upon the quality of action and the force of performance. We are aware in modern times, how the wave signals sent out from earth are received by the communication satellites, which send back the required data to earth. Obviously the reaction from the nearby surroundings returns to the doer more quickly but takes a longer time to come back from far off distances. This shows how an action performed has its reaction on the doer. The action spreads its influence in the entire cosmos, and in return, the reaction of the deed influences the doer however small the extent may be.

Maharishi gives the example of a letter sent by a man to his father, being redirected to his address, if the father is not in the home and if he has gone to another town. If he is not found even there, it will be again redirected to his new address. The letter will be repeatedly redirected as long as the father is traceable. If the father is no longer traceable and if his son, or nearest relation should be traced, the letter will go to the heir. Maharishi says that blood relation is the agency through which the reaction reaches the doer.

If an action is performed by an individual now, of which the influence will reach the doer in a thousand years, that influence will reach that soul wherever in the universe it may be. Maharishi says, that this philosophy of karma cannot be easily understood by those, who do not understand the philosophy of rebirth and continuity of life after death.

As long as the soul is not liberated and has not merged itself into the cosmic existence, so long, the individual jiva will continue to exist as an individual entity and will hold its individuality in whatever world or body it may be. It will continue to maintain its individuality and will receive the fruits of karma that it has done in the past.

Maharishi points out that the force of karma is such that even if the individual is liberated and his individuality has merged into cosmic existence, the influence of the karma done by him, will be received by his son, or grandson, or by those having blood affinity with him. But the reaction will never die and become nil. It will be carried on and on. If no one is left in the family, then its influence will go to the nearest of his blood relations—their friends and connections. The nature of karma is such, that the karma, the reaction, or the fruit of action unfailingly reaches the doer, just as a calf reaches its own mother in a herd of a thousands cows. Even if there is a large number of cows the calf will go to its own mother.

The philosophy of karma further explains, that whatever a man is, it is the result of his own past. None other than himself, is responsible for a man's happiness or suffering. If a man enjoys it is due to his own doings. If he suffers, it is due to his own actions.

To go into the question of the influence of karma, and to know how it effects the individual is beyond the scope of the human mind. Knowing this philosophy of karma, it behaves on every individual, to be good, and have only good intentions, and do only good things in life. The question naturally arises what is good and what is bad. Roughly speaking, society and the laws governing one's country tell us regarding good and bad to guide our actions. Going deeper into the values of good and bad, we find that a knowledge of the scriptures of our religions tell us, what is good and bad. The great truth is present in the scriptures of all religions and they represent the age old wisdom of the race transmitted to us by our fore-fathers and can be taken as an authority on what is good and what is bad. The culture and traditions represent an essence of an enduring good of society. How to get at an absolute standard of right and wrong? How to know what is virtuous and what represents evil? Maharishi examines these questions further.

Any action that creates a good influence for the doer in the present and secures good in the future, and which creates a good influence in all fields of the surroundings, is certainly a good action. Any action which produces a life supporting influence for the doer, in the present and future, and which exerts the same good influence for all the surroundings is called an act of virtue, a good action, a virtuous deed. Any action which produces a life damaging influence for the doer, either in the present, or in the future, and exerts the same life damaging influence on the surroundings, or, on any level of life in creation, is termed bad, wrong, sinful and immoral. Thus the action should result in all good to the doer and to the universe, for the present and for all time. This is the absolute standard of what is good and bad.

Any action done by the doer will have an influence not only on the doer, and at the present time alone. It influences the present and the future of the doer, and the whole universe. It is hard for us to find out what influence an action of a man will have at a particular time and at a particular stratum of the universe. Neither it is possible for us to know the reaction which it produces at any particular time in the present or in the future, at any particular level of creation.

The range of influence of an action pervades all limits of time, space and causation. The whole phenomenon of action and reaction is so complicated that it is beyond all limits of human comprehension. The influence of karma is beyond the scope of the human mind, and to know what is right and what is wrong, what action is worthy of performance, and what action is worthy of rejection, is beyond the scope of the human intellect. It seems impossible to know precisely, and understand what is right and what is wrong, on an intellectual basis, and to know right or wrong becomes highly complicated. Maharishi says, that it does seem possible to adjust the stream of life in such a way, that every action done by an individual is naturally good or right action. We shall examine, how the whole stream of life could be so adjusted that every thought, word and action of an individual, will naturally prove to be good for the doer, and produce a good and life sustained influence for the entire cosmos.

We know that the life of the universe involves its sustained maintenance and its steady growth in evolution. The maintenance and evolution of the multiple creation in the innumerable strata of the universe is carried on by a natural, automatic process based on the natural laws. We have seen previously that these laws function on the basis of the one eternal, never changing cosmic law, which ever maintains the integrity of the ultimate absolute existence. All the laws of nature, rigid in their character continue to function on different planes and maintain and evolve all beings. The whole cosmic process of evolution is thus carried on by the laws of nature, which ultimately are based on the cosmic law.

If it would be possible for us to bring the life stream of an individual to the plane of cosmic law, then, the entire process of the life of the individual and its progress and evolution would then be carried on naturally and automatically in accordance with the laws of nature. If therefore, we can find out a way, to systematize and regulate one's life to make it run in accordance with the laws of nature, then, all thought, speech, and action of the individual would produce an influence according to the laws of nature, working for the maintenance and evolution of all beings.

We have seen that by the regular practice of Transcendental Meditation, the mind of the individual can be brought in tune with the transcendental absolute pure consciousness, which is the plane of the cosmic law. Then, every action of the individual will produce a life supporting influence for the doer and the surroundings, and will be an act of virtue.

Maharishi says, that such a finding brings hope for every man in the world that an opportunity is open to him to tune his life in accordance with the laws of nature and sustain his progress and evolution. By thus doing, he will be producing through his thought, word and action and influence of good for himself and for all others; for the present and for all times.

The philosophy of karma therefore reveals to us, its unlimited scope and its ever increasing influence for the doer. The range of the fruit of action is far beyond the reach of the human mind's understanding. But, Maharishi says, by the performance of the action (Karma) of Transcendental Meditation, we can put ourselves on a plane of life where, anything done by us will naturally be in harmony and rhythm with cosmic life, and will be helpful to the maintenance and evolution of all beings all over the universe. This is a way, that an individual by being all good, will be able to do all good, says Maharishi.

By the practice of Transcendental Meditation being is brought out from the transcendental field to the field of relative existence and becomes infused into the nature of the mind. Karma done becomes a karma of absolute righteousness.

The important question that arises is, as to how the doer of Karma, will be free from the binding influence of karma. Maharishi analyses this question further.

Being is unmanifested in its nature, but karma is manifested. It is karma that makes being to manifest. Unmanifested Being transcendental and absolute in it's essential nature, is opposed to the nature of karma, which is temporary and perishable. Being is pure consciousness of absolute nature. Karma is based on conscious mind. On account of karma, the pure consciousness of being appears as conscious mind. Being is eternal unity in its nature; karma by its action makes the unity diversified in the multiple creation. Thus we find that the nature of karma is opposed to the nature of Being. Karma thus challenges the validity of being. This is the fundamental relationship between being and karma. We have seen previously that in the case of an experience by the experiencer, that the essential nature of the mind which is being is overshadowed by the experience. This overshadowing of the essential nature of the mind is said to be the binding influence of action of karma.

With the practice of Transcendental Meditation however the mind of the doer of karma is fully infused with the value of Being and the karma by the doer fails to overshadow the essential nature of the mind of the doer. The doer is then said to remain unbound by the doing, and the action is said not to bind the doer. This is how by gaining being at the level of the mind, karma fails to bind.

It is not possible to do away with Karma. Action has to be done because life means activity and the very nature of life is dynamic. It is therefore physically impossible to avoid karma or to escape from the action. Unless being shines into the nature of the mind, we cannot escape being bound by the action and its fruits.

Freedom from karma is gained by gaining the status of eternal being. By the action of Transcendental Meditation, it is possible for us to create a situation within ourselves, so that we will naturally be doing good for ourselves and creating good influences on the entire universe. at the same time it is possible for us to rise above the binding influence of action, and live a life of eternal freedom on earth. This then, is the philosophy of karma, which, not only deals with right and wrong and the far reaching influence of action, but also suggests a technique to rise above the binding influence of karma and live a life in freedom. The strength of an action depends primarily upon the strength of thought. To produce a powerful result and enjoy the great fruit of our action, it is necessary tot make the mind to the field of being. This is secured by the practice of Transcendental Meditation, which infuses being into the nature of the mind, so that, the conscious mind is always full with the value of being. When the mind is infused with the power of being, the creativity of the mind is infinitely great and at the expense of very little energy, very powerful actions may be performed to bring in the desired fruits. Karma or action done from the level of being, brings out maximum result for the doer and for the world. It fulfills the life purpose and produce beneficial influences of peace and harmony in the surroundings. It will have a life supporting effect on the entire universe.

The purpose of life is to be in bliss consciousness and evolve to the eternal state of liberation. It is to accomplish, achieve, and enjoy the maximum in life, and do the maximum good to oneself and to others and rise to a state of eternal freedom. These are the objectives to be attained by an individual. The philosophy of karma teaches us, how , by taking our attention to the field of transcendental being, we can fulfill not only the purpose of our life, but also, the purpose of cosmic evolution.

Karma or action done by the mind, which has not practiced Transcendental Meditation is motivated by selfish desires. In such a case, the karma done mayor may not be right for the doer. It may, or may not be right for the entire universe. Such a karma binds the mind and the mind remains bound by this karma and by its fruits. Such a karma is weak and needs great effort for its accomplishment. It brings great tension into the individual life and the surroundings.

Maharishi says, that, whatever be the aim of karma, there is only one technique of successful karma which produces the most affective, most powerful, and best results. That is to draw the mind within, to reach the field of transcendental being, and while returning, think of doing the action and come out to perform the action. The action will thus be strong and good. The fruit of such an action will thus be strong and good. The fruit of such an action will be gratifying on all levels. At the same time, neither the action, nor the fruits of action will bind the doer. The doer will be eternally free, performing the action in freedom, and enjoying the results in freedom, and producing the maximum good for himself and for others.

This is the philosophy of karma which finds its fulfillment in the simple practice of Transcendental Meditation.

Hence whatever be the activity, or whatever be the karma performed by the mind, senses, body or the surroundings, being is eternally maintained. This is said to be the art or technique of being with regard to Karma. Even though karma by nature is opposed to being, karma itself, is brought to the level of being. Being is ever maintained at the level of the mind, and therefore karma fails to challenge its validity. When both karma and being, are maintained at the level of the mind, then, this is said to be the skill of being and karma. In such a state, karma and being, both find their fulfillment simultaneously, in the regular practice of Transcendental Meditation.

Physiological Effects of Transcendental Meditation:

Maharishi then deals with the physiological effects of Transcendental Meditation.

It is found, during Transcendental Meditation, when the attention is drawn to consciously experience the subtler states of a thought, respiration becomes greatly reduced in amplitude, and the breathing becomes soft and refined. Physiologically it is clear that for this to happen, there must be a fall in the level of carbon-dioxide in the plasma. This can occur only as a result of either forced over breathing, which washes the carbon-dioxide out thought the lungs, or by a fall in the production of carbon-dioxide through the metallic process.

Since there is no forced over-breathing during Transcendental Meditation, we can only conclude that the softening of the breath is due to the fall in the production of carbondioxide by the metabolic process. Most of the energy for activity in the body involves basically the oxidation of carbon and then its elimination as carbondioxide. This shows that, when lesser amount of carbondioxide is eliminated due to softer breathing during Transcendental Meditation, the process of oxidation is lessened, and this naturally produces a lesser amount of energy.

On account of this reason, the activity of the body and that of the nervous system is reduced during Transcendental Meditation. Hence during Transcendental Meditation, as the mind proceeds to experience the subtler states of a thought, the whole body becomes calm and quiet.

Maharishi says, that this quieting of the body naturally gives an unusual degree of rest to the body and mind, and stores energy to a considerable degree. It is certain that the activity of the mind and the nervous system is least in this state, and thus, the mind becomes quiet and clams. Maharishi here points out the necessity of meditation in the life of a man, to bring the mind and the nervous system to a state of much needed restful alertness everyday. Here is what he say, "if by means of meditation, one does not produce this state, even for a few minutes daily, then, one has no chance of providing any rest to the inner machinery of the body, which otherwise, is kept functioning twenty four hours of the day for the whole of one's life as long as the breath keeps flowing.

Obviously, it is to the advantage of health and longevity of life that the ever functioning inner machinery of the body is allowed a few moments of rest and silence each day through the regular practice of Transcendental Meditation. (Page 194 Foot Note—Science of Being and Art of Living-T.M).

Speaking about the quiet state of restful alertness of the nervous system gained during Transcendental Meditation, Maharishi points out that in this quiet state, the mind and the nervous system are alertly poised like an arrow drawn fully back upon the bow; they are without activity, but the entire system is alert in stillness, and at the same time, all the mechanisms of the body are acutely balanced and steady. He further points out that this state of restful alertness of the nervous system, is its most healthy state, and is the basis of all energy and action. It is further said, that this state of restful alertness of the nervous system is a state of suspension wherein the nervous system is neither active nor passive. This state of no activity and no passivity is the state of being. The nervous system thus coming in tune with being, reaches a level of limitless energy and eternal existence of being. It is like the whole tree coming in tune with the field of its nourishment. In this state of restful alertness, the nervous system gains the most normal healthy state, which provides the key to good health.

The fall in carbondioxide output has been stated to have another effect, namely, the tendency to change the reaction of the blood from acidity toward alkalinity. This, in turn, is said to have widespread effect upon the blood chemistry all of which are beneficial to the whole system as a whole.

The system of Transcendental Meditation, as Maharishi, says, has proved beneficial in the field of health in two ways, its effects being both preventive and curative. The beneficial effects are :

1. It has proved to be a means of preserving mental and physical health.
2. It is found to provide complete rest and relaxation to the body and mind, restores energy and serves as an aid in medical treatment towards a speedy recovery from ill-health.

By body is meant the entire nervous system and all the limbs that are said to be the end organs of the nervous system.

It is know that the activity of the body depends upon the activity of the metabolic process and activity belongs to the relative field, while being is of transcendental absolute nature. The maintenance of the body depends upon both the subtle and gross fields of activity. If we could bring the body to a state where its activity stops, but the nervous system would not be allowed to be passive, but be in a state where it was neither active, nor passive, the activity of the body would then be on the level of being. If the metabolic process could just remain still without making the body passive, it would place the activity of the body on the level of being.

Maharishi then examines what is meant by the level of being. Being is the essential constituent of the individual. It is everything and in its unmanifested state forms the basis of everything and every phenomenon. It is the basis of all mind and matter. It is the basis of the entire manifest creation. This state of being is out of all relative existence. That is why, it is called transcendental and absolute. Maharishi explains the two terms, transcendental and absolute thus. Transcendental, because, it is out of all relative creation, absolute, because, it does not belong to the relative existence. It is never changing, eternal existence. Like the sap in a tree, being is omnipresent in creation. It is the ultimate source of all energy, intelligence, creativity and activity. It is itself, neither active, nor passive but it is the source or the fountain head of all activity and passivity.

In the relative field of life, it is seen that there is activity or passivity. Absolute being in its essential nature does not belong either to the field of activity or to the field of activity or to the field of passivity. Maharishi further points out that any state of life, which belongs to neither activity, nor passivity, goes out of relative existence, and naturally belongs to the field of absolute being. What belongs to the field of absolute being, gains the status of absolute being itself. For, nothing other than itself can be it. From the above, it is clear that the state of life, which is neither active, nor passive, belongs to the field of absolute being.

We know when the nervous system is active it is an awareness in the waking state. When the body becomes fatigued, the awareness is lost giving rise to deep sleep, and awareness may be said to be in a passive state. Hence it could be said that awareness depends upon the state of the nervous system. When the nervous system is active in the wakeful state, the mind has no opportunity to dissociate itself from the outside world activity. When the nervous system is tired, the mind has no chance of using the consciousness capacity, and loses its awareness in deep sleep.

If the nervous system could be brought to a state where it is able to hold the mind in such a way, that it is not able to use its conscious capacity for the experience of any outer object, while at the same time, it does not completely lose its conscious state—that is, if the mind could remain just conscious, without being conscious of anything in the outer world, then, in such a state, the mind will acquire the state of pure awareness, where the mind will be neither active nor passive in its nature. This pure awareness will be on the level of being, the transcendental reality.

If the nervous system could thus be established in the state, which is neither active, nor passive, but in a state of restful alertness, there would certainly be produced a condition for awareness on the plane of being.

In such a state of the nervous system, the relative and absolute states of life met and the nervous system then would be on the plane of being, or, being would be brought to the level of the nervous system.

How could such a state of the nervous system, the relative and absolute states of life meet and the nervous system then would be on the plane of being, or being would be brought to the level of the nervous system.

How could such a state of the nervous system be produced ? Maharishi answers this question thus. Physiologically, the functioning of the nervous system depends upon the metabolic process, and the metabolic process depends upon breathing. If by some means, breathing could be slowed down, made softer, or reduced in amplitude, the metabolic process would thereby be reduced. Further, if the breathing could be brought to a state where it was neither active, nor passive, then, that would be the state of extremely delicate breath, where the breath could be said to be flowing, and yet, not flowing. Then, that would be the state, where metabolism would be established in a state of suspension, between activity and no activity on the level of being. Such a state would harmonise the body with being. In this state life would be sustained, but its expression would be silent in the relative existence, says Maharishi.

In this state of the nervous system the mind would be kept awake in itself, and with reference to this state of self awareness of the mind, the whole body would be sustained in itself. According the Maharishi, this state represents a state of no physical change in the body, and the whole structure and all the matter of the body will just be suspended on the level of the pure state of life. Further, this is a state where no physical change in the body will exist and the whole physical structure and all matter of the body, will just be suspended on the level of the pure state of life. Maharishi puts it as a state, where the process of evolution, or the process of change, has stopped building up, or deteriorating and the change has ceased to be. In such a state the whole body as also the mind have both been placed on the level of being. Regarding this state Maharishi points out, "Mind and matter both, forming the gross and subtle aspects of the individual, have been raised tone level of never changing existence, the level of eternal absolute being. Here they lie together in unity with one another, for, both have gained the same level of life". (Page 197-Science of Being and Art of Living—T.M.).

Hindu tradition speaks of life immortal (chiranjivi) enjoyed by the seven ancient legendary figures, Ashwatthama, Bali, Vyasa, Hanuman, Vibhishana, Kripa and Parashurama who it is said had mastered the technique for the eternal longevity of life. These legendary figures are believed by Hindus to be living even to this day.

Maharishi says, if there is any hesitation in accepting the notion that in this suspended state of never changing existence, the mind and body are united in one state of life, at least, there should be no hesitation in accepting the statement, that in this suspended state, body and mind are in perfect co-ordination with each other. The individual mind is then one with pure consciousness or absolute intelligence and the body in this state of perfect health is resting in full accord with the mind.

Thus it is seen that, by reducing the breath, it should be possible to set the nervous system in the state of perfect health, and at the same time, in full coordination with the mind. Such a perfect state with regard to body and mind and their mutual relationship is only possible, on the level of being. And it is possible only, when either the mind is brought to the level of being, or the body is brought to the level of being.

Maharishi categorises the following ways by which desired results could be achieved.

1. Psychological—where only the mind is involved. This in practice, is the system of Transcendental Meditation
2. Physiological—where metabolic process is reduced by working on the body or breathing. This practice is achieved though yogic physical culture and proper breathing exercises.
3. Psycho-physiological—here both mind and breathing are made to function on their levels in order to bring both the mind and body to that state of suspension of the level of being.

Method o bringing breathing to a state of neither activity nor passivity :

The state of breath has to be created in a natural way. Any unnatural method will cause strain. It cannot be done by attempting to slow the breath, because slowing will strain the process of breathing. One possibility for slowing the breath is the extended practice of controlled breathing, so that, the system becomes used to maintaining itself either when the breath is in, or out. This practice does result in maintaining the body with very soft breathing. Eventually a physiological state is created in the system in which, the breath is brought to a condition of neither activity nor passivity. Maharishi points out that such a practice of controlled breathing results in bringing the body on the level of being. But it requires long practice and a great amount of control is necessary for achieving success through this path. He therefore says that this path is not suitable for the householder's way of life, and is even less suited to the busy householder of the modern nuclear age.

Maharishi considers another way to achieve the state through slowing of breath. The principles involved in this second way are summarized below.

By experience we know that breathing is faster when we run, and becomes slower when we sit. Breathing becomes faster after we have eaten because, more oxygen is needed for the digestion of the food. It is therefore clear that breathing is slow or fast according to work to be done by the body. The work to be done by the body depends upon how the mind wants the body to function. Therefore the activity of the body which directly controls the process of breathing is governed by the process of thinking.

It has been previously shown while analyzing the thought process, that the thought process on the level of the conscious mind is the result of much greater activity, than it is, at the starting point of thought. Increased activity naturally needs greater release of energy in the system, thus necessitating correspondingly heavier breathing. If instead, the thought could be consciously recognized as a thought right at the source itself, then, the energy required to raise the thought to the ordinary conscious level of the mind would naturally be saved, and would involve less production of every in the system. This would necessitate a fall in the process of oxidation in the plasma, which in turn, would soften the breathing, and the goal of bringing the breath to a state of neither activity nor passivity will thus be achieved.

From the above, it is clear that, as the mind begins to experience the subtler states of thought during Transcendental Meditation, it engages itself in correspondingly less activity and consequently, lesser release of energy in the system. As a result of this, breathing simultaneously begins to be shallower, more refined and reduced in amplitude. When the mind arrives at the experience of the subtlest state of thought, the breathing arrives at the shallowest level of its flow. Ultimately, when the mind transcends the subtlest thought and gains the level of pure consciousness, the breathing comes to that state which is neither active nor passive, the level of pure Being. Regarding this state at the level of pure Being Maharishi states, "Thus we find that the practice of bringing the mind to the level of Being, simultaneously brings the breath to the same level and establishes the nervous system and the body in the plane of absolute existence. In this state there would be no release of energy by the metabolic process, no change, or decay in the state of the body. The body, then, becomes the fit medium for omnipresent absolute Being to shine through, and radiate Being in the relative field". (Page 199-Science of Being and Art of Living-T.M.)

Maharishi gives the example of a glass of water placed in the sun. the sun gets reflected in it. The sun always there, but it shows no reflection, unless a proper medium is there, through which, it can get reflected. Similarly Being is always here, there, and everywhere, but it has no opportunity to radiate itself directly in the relative existence, until, a suitable state in the nervous system is created. By bringing the nervous system to this condition, through, (i) systematic refinement of breathing, or (ii) thinking or (iii) both together, the body can be brought to the level of Being to live long in good health.

We have seen previously, that the regular practice of Transcendental Meditation, where the mind is brought to the level of Being, simultaneously brings the breath to the same level and establishes the nervous system and the body in the plane of absolute existence, and contributes for the maintenance of good health, serenity of mind and longevity of life.

PART III

Towards Life in freedom

Life in Freedom:

Maharishi explains, that for life to be lived in freedom, all the different components of life should function in full co-ordination with one another and they should fulfill their ultimate purpose of gaining a state of eternal absolute freedom, in divine bliss consciousness.

Freedom in life should mean that life in all its planes of physical, mental and spiritual existence should be full, unrestricted, unbounded, and complete for all values. In the physical plane it should mean that the surroundings should be conducive to the fulfillment of life.

The body should enjoy perfect health. There should be perfect mutual co-ordination in the functioning of its components so that, there is no distraction from the purpose of life, or obstruction to the flow of individual life.

The state of freedom from bondage is gained by the mind, body and surrounding with the regular practice of Transcendental Meditation. So long as the mind is not functioning with its full potentialities, by using all the faculties it has, latent and conscious, the freedom of the mind will be restricted. A state of full unfoldment of the latent potentialities of the mind is the first step towards gaining the freedom for the mind.

It has been previously observed that the mind achieves the ability to function with a fully developed conscious capacity, by the regular practice of Transcendental Meditation.

Another important point regarding the freedom of the mind according to Maharishi, is the freedom from the bondage of experience. Unless the mind becomes fee from the bondage of experience, it cannot obtain the liberation in life. On this point the whole philosophy of bondage of experience and liberation of life depends.

Maharishi points out that this point of liberation from the bondage of experience, has been very widely misunderstood for the past many centuries by the metaphysicists, and he attributes this misunderstanding of the phenomenon of experience, as being responsible for the loss of the direct path to freedom and liberation in life. He emphasizes that the phenomenon of experience forms the main field of metaphysical study, an it is only a correct understanding of this phenomenon of experience, that provides a direct way to eternal liberation of life. It is pointed out by him that this long-standing misconception has been responsible for the failure of students of metaphysics to locate the essential nature of the divine Being, and thus liberate themselves from the clutches of bondage of karma.

Maharishi analysis the phenomenon of experience. The process of experience of an object entails the image of the object traveling to the retina of the eye and reaching the mind. The image of the object coming on to the mind gives the experience of the object. The result of the experience apart from the sight of the object is that the mind, as it receives the impression of the objection is that the mind, as it receives the impression of the object is overshadowed by that impression. The mind's essential nature, which is being, is as if lost, and therefore only the image of the object remains impressed on the mind. Maharishi says "The seer of the mind is as though lost in the sight".

It is seen from the above that the essential nature of the subject, or the experiencer within, is lost in the experience of the object. It is as though the object had annihilated the subject, or the experiencer within. The subject, or the experiencer, or the mind, misses the experience of its own essential nature, its Being, while engaged in the experience of the object. The object only remains in the consciousness. This is what the common experience of people is.

When the experience thus holds the object in predominance, and the subject loses itself in the object, the subject is said to be in bondage by the object.

Maharishi says, that the values of the object have bound or overshadowed the nature of the subject, and have become predominant, leaving no trace of the essential nature of the subject. This is bondage of the subject; in the metaphysical field is termed as the identification of the subject with the object.

He examines this question further. On the basis of the above logic, one may come to the conclusion that identification of the object itself, is the nature of the bondage. Maharishi says that such a conclusion is erroneous and has proved highly damaging. Thinkers and philosophers in the past, who guided the destiny of metaphysical thought for many centuries, advocated practices for gaining freedom from bondage, which have proved highly damaging and unproductive to the lives of seekers of truth. In the past, metaphysicians and great thinkers concluded, that identification is the nature of the bondage. Such a conclusion which was incorrect took the people away from God realization.

If identification of the subject with the object was considered bondage, then naturally, attaining freedom was thought to be in terms of non-identification. It was therefore thought, that, if one does not identify himself with the object of experience, then, one would be in the state of freedom. This erroneous metaphysical understanding, has given rise to various practices of gaining freedom. Those that attempted to gain freedom by trying to maintain self-awareness or God remembrance, or God consciousness, while being engaged in worldly action, took to these practices with all sincerity. The net result was fatal. Trying to maintain self-awareness of God, or God consciousness on the level of thinking, and at the same time engaging oneself in activity, only divided the mind. This practice of dividing the mind made the mind weak. Life's activity suffered, because, it did not receive the full concentration of the mind. Self-consciousness, or divine, or God consciousness, remained only an act on the gross conscious thinking level of the mind. The aspirant was found to be neither fully in the field of activity, nor fully in the state of God consciousness. The long practice of dividing the mind in this way resulted in the weakening of the personality. Those who did so, neither cultivated self consciousness, nor God consciousness, nor were they successful in the world.

When practical people in society found that the life of such people devoted to God, or God consciousness was found to be half in the world, and half out, they were afraid to start such practices of spiritual unfoldment, because, they saw those that were devoted to such practices were found weak in practical life and less dynamic, and at the same time they never realized God consciousness either.

Maharishi enunciates the following conclusions on the basis of his thesis on experience.

1. A though of freedom although it seems to be good, is only a thought and not a state.
2. A thought of freedom is as much binding as any other thought.
3. Thought by its very nature is out of oneself.
4. When the mind begins to entertain a thought, it comes into the field of duality, and the thought overshadows the essential nature of the mind.
5. Therefore, any thought causes identification.
6. The problem of identification was thus not at all solved by the thought of the self, or of the divine, or of God.

That is why, practices which had as their core, the thought of the self, or of the divine, or God, failed to give freedom from bondage to the people and the quest for freedom remained unsatisfied and became confused by such practices which involved the idea of the divine self, or God on the thinking level only.

Maharishi in his thesis points out the fundamental error in these practices, wherein, it was thought that the identification itself was considered to be bondage. He further says that identification is not, and can never be bondage. What is bondage is the inability to maintain Being, namely the transcendental reality, along with identification. Therefore bondage is the inability to maintain Being, while indulging in the field of experience and activity. If identification were bondage, then, freedom would be possible only in the state after death. It is only after death, one ceases to experience and ceases to be active. So long as one is alive, one has to continue to experience and act and so, it is impossible to avoid identification during one's life time.

Therefore identification can never be considered bondage, because, one has to be in the world, and freedom has to be lived in the world, and living in the world means identifying oneself with everything for the sake of experience and activity.

There is nothing in identification as such, that the seekers of truth and aspirants of reality should be afraid of. What is needed is, that a state of mind has to be cultivated, so that the mind when engaged with outer things of life, does not overshadow the pure state of Being.

The maintenance of Being at the level of the mind can never be achieved by the practice of thinking about Being. Being can be spontaneously lived on the level of thought, only when, the very nature of the mind is transformed into the nature of Being. Then all experiences will be on the level of Being. Maharishi emphasizes that only then, will it be possible that experience will not be able to overshadow, or overthrow, the validity of Being. Then Being will be lived along with identification.

Maharishi further observes in his thesis that, if one thinks about Being, it is just a thought of Being, and not the state of Being. To establish Being in the very nature of the mind, so that, during the waking, dreaming, or deep sleep states, and through all the experiences of activity and inactivity in life, Being is maintained and not obstructed, and continues to be, it is necessary that the mind is transformed into the nature of Being.

To achieve this, the mind should gain familiarity with the state of Being to such a degree, that the mind lives Being, through all the situations and conditions of life. This is made possible by making the conscious mind, pass through in a systematic manner, the subtle states of experience of thinking, and then making it transcend the subtlest state of thought, to arrive eventually at the transcendental state of Being. When, from this transcendental state, the mind comes out into the relative field of existence, the mind emerges familiar with the state of pure Being. Thus, through the regular practice of Transcendental Meditation, the nature of the Being becomes steadfast, or firmly established in the very nature of the mind to such an extent, that it can never be obscured or overshadowed, by any of the experiences of the relative order.

This permanent infusion of the absolute bliss consciousness into the nature of the mind establishes the mind in the state of everlasting freedom, and when the mind identifies itself with the objects of experience, or engages itself with the activity, Being and freedom, continue to exist along with the experience and activity.

This is the state of eternal freedom, which cannot be obstructed or obscured, or overshadowed by any state of experience, activity or passivity of the relative existence. This is the state of a 'Stithapragna' as it is termed in Hindu Philosophical thought.

Thus, it is seen that freedom in life belongs to the field of Being, or transcendental reality. Regarding this Maharishi says, "It can be established only through the practice of Transcendental Meditation, which establishes pure Being in the very nature of the mind by taking the mind to the field of the transcendent". (Page 236-Science of Being and Art of Living-T.M.)

From the above, it is clear, that Being, or Divine or God is something to be lived.

Maharishi further contends that a mere fanciful thought of it does not much help in practical life. We can cherish a thought of God in our mind. It may provide a psychological satisfaction to us. But it doest not provide us with the advantage of living God, or of contact with the almighty God. A thought of God is only an abstract imagination. It is not a concrete state of God. This is the fundamental difference between really succeeding in establishing eternal freedom in life by attaining the state of God, and remaining in an intellectual mood of hovering in the thought of freedom of God. Here is what Maharishi says further, "Such misunderstanding in the field of metaphysics for the past many centuries has only helped to mislead the genuine seekers of Truth, and has created a great gulf between the spiritual and material aspects of life". (Page 236-Science of Being and Art of Living-T.M.)

We have seen previously that to gain freedom in God consciousness the mind has to be led to the filed of bliss consciousness. It is not attained by making a mood of it. Maharishi expresses his sorrow that realization of God consciousness, or eternal freedom on earth has remained only at the thinking level. Mystical practices in the name of enlightenment and God realization, have left the true aspirants in a state of suspension, in the mere thought of God. The thought of God, Maharishi says, swings the mind into the abstract, and the thought envelops the mind and the aspirant loses a clear conception of the outer surroundings, and feels that it is the state of God consciousness, that he has experience. Maharishi calls such an experience as sheer delusion.

Man has always thought that God is omnipresent and he is present everywhere. This has been the common understanding. Unless the mind is brought to the level of omnipresent Being, the omnipresence of God cannot be lived. Thinking of God, and the divine, has created a great obstacle in the field of metaphysics and religion, for the achievement of the state of God realization.

Maharishi points out, "It has only helped the people to remain as though suspended in the air, in the name of God". (Page 237-Science of Being and Art of Living-T.M.)

It is to be noted here that God realization, is a positive concrete experience on the level of pure existence. It is more real, more substantial, and more sublime than the existence of anything on earth. Through Transcendental Meditation the mind is led from the field of relative existence to God consciousness in the transcendental field, which is omnipresent, omniscient and omnipotent.

We have seen previously that the process is simple. When one puts his mind in the process, he experiences the subtler states, transcends the subtlest, and then comes back to the relative field. This occurs over and over again, morning and evening, within a short time a state of mind will be gained in which Being is not lost, even while the mind is engaged in the field of experience and activity. This is the state of real freedom in life.

What does such a state of real freedom in life mean for the human individual? In terms of achievement they can be summed up.

1. During the process of transcending the conscious capacity of the mind increases.

2. When one comes out of meditation into the relative field, and engages oneself in the field of experience and activity in the world, his experience of object becomes deeper, fuller, and more substantial.

3. One engages in all his activities with greater energy, more intelligence and improved efficiency.

4. This is said to be the glory of divine realization. When on the one hand, the state of Being is cultivated to remain for all times infused into the nature of the mind, on the other, the field of life's activity in the world becomes more substantial, and more rewarding on all levels. Such a state brings harmony between the inner spiritual, and outer material glories of life.

From times immemorial, such a goal of attaining the state of God consciousness, while actively engaging in the activities of the world, has been the supreme quest of man, and the scriptures of religions and the whole field of metaphysics have laid this supreme goal, as their eternal pursuit, because on the way to achieve this goal the world is made better, the efficiency and creativity of man improves, and the individual is transformed and his life glorified at all levels of his life. While enjoying the divine consciousness, he also enjoys the world on all levels of his activity. His mind becomes fixed in bliss consciousness, his experience and activity in the world become more profound, and being in bliss consciousness his creativity and intelligence assume their peak values. He becomes a God realized man, and he reaches the status of a successful man in the world. Maharishi says that the two states go hand in hand. Success in the divine quest brings the height of success in the world in a most natural way and the individual life is enriched virtually lives the full life in eternal freedom.

Acharya Shankara an intellectual giant, was a combination of philosopher, statesman and poet, a man of rare acumen and of profound learning and an inspired teacher and thinker. He stands among the greatest figures in the history of the world. He is the unrivalled profounder of adviata Vedanta, the non-dualistic aspect of vedic teachings. He has written commentaries on the Vedanta-sutras, the principal Upanishads, and the Bhagvad Gita and has produced major philosophical works. By his invaluable works, he has brought forth the immortal truths embodied in the ancient sacred texts of Hindu culture and has given solace and light to the sorrowful hearts of a large segment of mankind. His non-dualistic (adviata) Vedanta philosophy has been accepted as authoritative. The quintessence of his philosophy can be stated:

"Brahman is real, the world is unreal; the jiva is verily the Brahman and no other". Advaita Vedanta repudiates the ultimate reality of the world of experience, but not its empirical existence. Empirical experiences are valid, until the identity of the Self with Brahman is realized. The world of experience, which is referred to, as "Maya" exists in the relative phase of existence, while Brahman is the transcendental reality beyond time, space and causation. But behind all the relative world of diversity, lies the unmanifested attribute-less absolute existence, the Brahman of the Upanishads. Sri Maharishi

Mahesh Yogi in his book on Science of Being and Art of Living-T.M." has clearly brought out these two aspects of existence, as being the relative and the absolute, and has explained that they are the two different phases of one and same ultimate reality.

It is to the credit of Sri.Maharishi Mahesh Yogi in the contemporary world, that he has shown by the introduction of his system of Transcendental Meditation based on the philosophy of the Upanishads and traditions of Shankaracharya, a practical method suitable for everyone, to attain the state of the transcendental reality and remain in eternal freedom, while being fully engaged in life's activities. Sri Maharishi, has in a way bridged the wide chasm that separated spirituality and material life of man for the past many centuries and even to the present day.

He has shown, how a man by regularly practicing Transcendental Meditation can ever remain established in Being in the State of eternal freedom, while being engaged in life's activities. In the present day world, Maharishi's contribution seems to be the greatest to mankind, and in this respect Sri.Maharishi's position remains unique and unsurpassed in the contemporary world. His method of Transcendental Meditation has caught the imagination of all scientific thinkers in the west, and has been readily accepted as a method to relieve stress, mental tension and worry in the modern busy world.

Maharishi has based his philosophy on the philosophy of the Upanishads. His Being, corresponds to the 'Brahman' of the Upanishads. He has brought 'Being' within the realm of actual experience. By practicing regularly Transcendental Meditation, man's mind can remain firmly established in the transcendental reality even while he engages himself in all the activities of life using his full potential. He has shown to the world the practical way to attain the state of the transcendental Being. We have already discussed how Maharishi differentiates the absolute reality from the relative phenomenon of life. Man exists in this world of reality in the relative state, while his inner self is the absolute transcendental, which is the reservoir of all power, creative energy and intelligence. The simple method of the technique of Transcendental Meditation practiced regularly, twenty minutes in the morning, and twenty minutes in the evening, makes possible the establishment of the transcendental Being, in the nature of the mind. Man then begins to live the transcendental reality in his actual life, in a state of eternal freedom. This seems to be the greatest contribution which Maharishi has given out to the contemporary world, for man to live a fully potential life, free from tension, worry, and strain and at the same time enjoying the state of eternal freedom.

PART IV

Fulfillment

Fulfillment of Life:

Maharishi defines fulfillment of life as attaining the status of divine life and living the life of eternal freedom, while at the same, time living the fullness of all values of human existence.

Man should live the bliss consciousness of the absolute transcendental Being, along with the relative joys of the variety of creation. They should be lived hand in hand. This would mean that man will be living the fulfillment of life in cosmic consciousness.

During Transcendental Meditation, the conscious mind arrives at the transcendental field of the absolute Being which is of unmanifested nature. Here, in this field, the mind will have transcended all relativity and will be in the state of the absolute reality. All limits of experience of thought will have been transcended. The mind will be left all by itself in the state of pure consciousness. This state of pure consciousness or this state of absolute pure being is called self consciousness.

When this self consciousness is not lost, even when the mind comes out of the transcendental field and engages itself in activity in the relative field, then, self consciousness gains the status of cosmic consciousness. The self consciousness is then eternally established in the nature of the mind. It is naturally maintained, even when the mind is awake, dreaming or in deep sleep states. It is then said to be cosmic consciousness.

This state of cosmic consciousness includes the experience of the relative field along with the state of transcendental Being. It is state where the mind lives in eternal freedom, while at the same time it remains unbound by the experience during the activity of the relative world. In this state there will be no bondage of experience and the mind will be in a state of eternal freedom, while experiencing the relative states of life-waking, dreaming, or sleeping.

The individual will then enjoy perfect mental and physical health, and the divine intelligence speaks in all the phases of his life. God consciousness permeates all the experiences and activities of life. It will be a state of integrated life where all the planes of living are infused with divine consciousness and overflow with universal love. In such a state life finds its fulfillment in the unbounded ocean of divine wisdom. A man with cosmic consciousness will bring out unbounded, unlimited amount of love overflowing in all directions for everything. This ability of fulfillment comes with the constant practice of Transcendental Meditation, and then the person turns to devote himself to God.

Speaking about devotion Maharishi says, "Unless the state of cosmic consciousness is achieved, devotion in the real sense of the word does not begin; it does not mean much. A man whose heart doest not flow in universal love doest not gain much from devotion, because, devotion results in surrender, and surrender means loss of one's identity and the gaining of the identity of the beloved. The path of love, the path of devotion, is successfully traversed only by the cosmically evolved souls", (Page 249-Science of Being and Art of Living—T.M.)

Maharishi further points out that devotion and love belong in full value only to the life of cosmic consciousness. Regarding devotion he says, "Belong the level of cosmic consciousness the power of love and devotion is limited and insignificant, and therefore all those who want to follow the path of devotion are invited to start the practice of Transcendental Meditation, which enables the individual to rise to a state of cosmic consciousness without much struggle and strife". (Page 250-Science of Being and art of Living-T.M.)

The individual then comes in tune with the cosmic life. The movements of the individual are then in accord with the movements of the entire cosmos. The purpose of the individual is found in accord with the purpose of the entire cosmos. Then the life of the individual is found established in cosmic life, and becomes a part of the cosmic state of life.

He will then be a realized soul and everything that comes out of him will breathe the air of cosmic mind. He becomes the living expression of the Omnipresent, Omniscient, cosmic existence. This is the fulfillment of life.

Fulfillment of Religion:

"Religion" comes from the Latin root "religire", meaning "re", back, "ligire", to bind.

The Purpose of religion is to bind man back to his source, his origin.

The fulfillment of religion lies in gaining for man that for which the word religion itself stands. It lies in gaining for man a direct way to God realization. It should provides for making him a complete man, with fully integrated life, and his intelligence, creativity, wisdom peace and happiness all functioning with their maximum values.

The purpose of religion is fulfilled, if religion brings the body and mind's activity of man back to source of all activity. Mind is the pivot of life. If mind could be drawn back to its origin, the whole life would be drawn to its source and the purpose of religion would be fulfilled.

Religion should raise the consciousness of man to the level of God, or cosmic consciousness, and the mind of man should be raised to the level of divine intelligence or universal cosmic mind.

Religion should co-ordinate the individual life with cosmic life and should improve all values of human life. It is the practical way to realize the supreme reality which is brought to light by philosophy. Philosophy is speculative, but religion is practical and provides a direct way to God realization. It enables the human beings to evolve to the level of the Divine.

Maharishi has no kind words when he points out the deplorable state of religions in the world to-day. He says that the present day religion has only the body and is devoid of the spirit. Only the rituals and dogmas are found; the spirit has departed. He attributes this as the reason why the followers of religion do not find fulfillment. Maharishi doest not underrate the importance of religious rituals. He says that the dogmatic aspects of religion are necessary, because, for the soul to be, the body has to be. Rituals have the value in so far as they constitute the body of religion. They serve the main purpose of providing a proper field for the spirit of religion to guide the destiny of man. Maharishi gives the important place for the rituals. He says "All the rituals of the various religions are like the spirit. Both are necessary, they should go hand in hand. One will not survive without the other". (Page 252-Science of Being and Act of Living-T.M.)

Speaking about the religions of to-day, Maharishi points out, that they are in a state of decay, because they lack the spirit. He compares the religion of today to the corpse of a man without the inner spirit. The several rites and rituals practiced by people remain without elevating the people's consciousness. Maharishi laments that the inner spirit of religion does not seem to exist to-day. It has failed to capture the imagination of the modern man. Further, there is hardly any religion in the world to-day, which prescribes the practice of Transcendental Meditation as a practical method of raising the consciousness of man to the level of the experience of the transcendental reality. It is only by such direct experience of the transcendental reality that man will be convinced of the truth of God realization.

The possibility is available in the practice of Transcendental Meditation for the peoples of all religions to lead a state of integrated life by the direct experience of absolute consciousness of divine Being. Maharishi points out that mere suggestive teachings on the surface of the conscious mind do not have much to do, by way of transformation of the inner mind. Mere teaching truthfulness, kindness, love for others and fear of God by the religions have failed to elevate man and have not provided any significant degree of evolution of human life, because a practical technique of raising the consciousness to the divine value has not been used.

So long as man remains at the human level, he is apt to err. It is necessary to take him above the field of error, bring the divine intelligence within the range of the conscious mind, and thereby infuse the divine nature into the nature of man.

Transcendental Meditation is the practice to live everything that the religions have been teaching through the ages. It is through this, that man readily rises to the level of divine Being. It is only this practice that brings fulfillment to all religions. Man by raising his consciousness to the level of the divine Being makes his life a life of fulfillment.

Fulfillment of Psychology:

According to Maharishi the following objectives have to be fulfilled by psychology: The mind must be made strong. The conscious capacity of the mind must be increased. Man must be made to use the full potential of the mind. It should help him in unfolding the latent faculties of the mind, and in bringing greater contentment, peace and happiness to the mind. It should increase the efficiency and creativity in the individual. The individual must be able to increase his power of concentration and will power, and be able to maintain his inner equanimity and peace, even while he is busily engaged in the worldly activities. He should develop self confidence, power of tolerance, clear thinking and greater power of thought. Finally, the individual's mind should be established in the state of eternal freedom and peace in God consciousness under all circumstances, in the midst of his activity in the relative field of existence.

Psychology will find its ultimate fulfillment only when the individual's mind is tuned itself and remains tuned, with the cosmic mind, and when every activity of the individual is in conformity with the cosmic evolution and is in co-ordination with the purpose of cosmic life.

Psychology should also aim at enabling a man to overcome the stress and strain produced by the failures or pressures of work in his day-to-day busy life. It should further give him such strength to the mind that it never fails him under stress and strain and never allows him to fall victim to what are called psychosomatic diseases.

The purpose of the study of psychology should be to enable man to overcome the obstacles in life and live without any suffering. It should provide him that strength of thought, force and clear thinking, which will enable him to fulfill his desires and live the life of fulfillment.

Further it is affirmed that the goal of psychology, the study of the mind, should be to enable man live all values of life, enjoy all phases of existence, live the maximum of life, and live a fulfilled life in eternal freedom in God consciousness.

Judged by these great possibilities in the field of psychology available for man to elevate his life in the direction of fulfillment, and reviewing the progress and achievement so far made by that science, Maharishi records that they are highly disappointing.

He records his disapproval to the methods adopted by the modern psycho-analysis which reminds a person that his past was miserable, or that his surroundings and circumstances were unfavourable, or that his associations were depressing or that there was lack of love and harmony with dear and near ones. He says that such information delivered to anyone by way of analyzing the past results in suppression of one's consciousness. He points out it is a crime to tell anyone that his individual life is based on the inefficient and degenerate influence of the environment of his past. The psychological influence of such depressing information is demoralizing. Speaking about this Maharishi observes. "The inner core of one's heart becomes twisted by such information. On the other hand information regarding the greatness of one's family traditions and glory of one's parents, friends and environment, helps to elevate one's consciousness and directly encourages one to surmount and rise above one's weaknesses" (Page 258- Science of Being and Art of Living-T.M.)

Maharishi disapproves the attempt of psychology to analyse the individual's way of thinking and bringing to the conscious level the buried misery of the past, even for the purpose of enabling him to see the cause of stress and suffering. He says such an attempt is highly deplorable, for it helps to strengthen directly the impressions of the miserable past and serves to suppress his consciousness in the present. He calls it as the blessing of God, that one normally forgets the past. He admits that the present is certainly born of the past, but equally so, is the fact, that the past has been through lesser developed states of consciousness, and that the present, belongs to a more developed state of life. Therefore, he argues, that it is only a loss to overshadow or eclipse the more evolved state at the present, with the memories of reviews of the less evolved past. Maharishi's remarks on this aspect are highly revealing. He says "the whole of one's past is less mature and tends towards the life of animals, and the result of digging out the buried impressions of lesser developed states is that the lesser developed states of animal life overshadow the brightness and brilliance of the developed human consciousness in the present" (Page 259- Science of Being and Art of Living-T.M.)

It is true that by looking into the past, one's vision gets expanded, but, even though it expands it brings to the conscious level the lesser developed states of life. Looking back to the past expands one's vision, but at the same time the vision of the past overshadows one's genius and brightness of intelligence and thereby suppresses the developed consciousness of the present.

Maharishi further points out that, if there could be a way to expand one's consciousness in the direction of more evolved states of consciousness, and if the present state of consciousness could be enlarged and led through these states, to the unbounded universal state of cosmic consciousness, that would be the way, whereby the subjects of psycho-analysis would certainly be saved from the unfortunate influence of overshadowing their consciousness, by digging into the mind of the miserable past. This aspect of Maharishi's thesis forms an important contribution, in the field of the study of psychology, and to the subject of psychoanalysis in particular. Maharishi makes a fervent appeal to the statesman of the various nations of the world to realize the degenerating influence of modern psychoanalysis and replace it with the practice of Transcendental Meditation.

The practice of Transcendental Meditation directly elevates the consciousness of the individual, and thereby, not only strengthens the mind of the individual, but also enables him to use his full potential, making him better, more powerful, peaceful, happy and creative.

It will bring modern psychology to fulfill its long cherished aim of glorifying man's life in all fields of existence.

Further, in the process of gaining transcendental consciousness, the subtle levels of thought are brought to the conscious level, and the whole thought process comes within the range of the conscious mind. The conscious capacity of the mind increases to the fullest scope of the mind, and the man gets the ability to rise up to his full mental potential in thought and action.

Further, the mind becoming familiar with the deeper levels of the thought process, becomes aware of the subtler levels of creation. Becoming familiar with these subtle regions of creation, it gains the ability to stimulate those regions for all advantage, to unfold the latent faculties of the mind. Having become familiar with all levels of creation, subtle and gross, the mind gets the ability to operate in the subtle regions in such a way as to bring advantages from the entire field of creation into the everyday life.

During Transcendental Meditation the absolute Being, which is the plane of cosmic law, comes within the range of the conscious capacity of the mind, and the mind is naturally put in tune with the cosmic law. When that happens, it is in tune with all the laws of nature. The flow of the mind is then in accordance with the natural stream of evolution, and will serve the cosmic purpose of life. This is how the practice of Transcendental Meditation establishes the mind in the state of cosmic mind.

Transcendental consciousness is bliss consciousness. When this bliss consciousness comes within the range of the conscious mind, the mind becomes contented on the basis of the positive experience of bliss. Then, on the basis of contentment, all virtues flourish. Love, kindness, compassion, tolerance and appreciation of others all naturally take hold of the mind. The individual then becomes the center of divine intelligence. Speaking about this aspect, Maharishi observes "The field of absolute Being, the field of pure consciousness, is the source of all intelligence, all creativity, all peace and happiness. When that field comes within the conscious range of the mind, the mind naturally becomes highly creative, greatly intelligent, filled with peace and contentment. These are the faculties that make a man accomplish all that he could possibly aspire for, in life. (Page 262- Science of Being and Art of Living- T.M.)

Maharishi claims that the practice of Transcendental Meditation provides the key to open the gates of the most advanced science of psychology which had been developed in ancient Indian and which finds it echo in the teachings of the Bhagavad-Gita.

Psychology as depicted in the Bhagavad-Gita represents clearly the study of how the human mind is carried in its development from the pitiable state of anxiety and depression, to that most highly developed state, wherein the individual's consciousness becomes one with the consciousness of the eternal Being thus representing the most evolved state of human evolution, one could aspire for.

Maharishi points out that the Bhagavad-Gita describes the psychologies of the individual and the cosmic mind, and marvelously succeeds in establishing a harmonious correlation between them. Thereby, the temporal phase of man becomes infused with the status of the eternal life divine. The Gita further points out, that, if this does not take place the individual is doomed for ever to remain subjected to the phenomenal aspects of nature and as a consequence, suffers perpetual bondage and suffering.

How the surroundings and circumstances will have an overwhelming influence on the mind of the individual has been clearly brought out at the very beginning of the text, in the case of the most highly evolved man. Arjuna, the greatest archer of his time, the hero of the Mahabharata. Although, being awake to a most complete knowledge of right and wrong in the world. Arjuna is unable to choose the right path and rise to the occasion before him. He falls into a state of utter indecision and dejection. The surroundings and circumstances had such an overbearing influence upon his mind, that all the persuasions and suggestions made by Lord Krishna were powerless and proved of no avail. Arjuna could not rise to the occasion, and come out of his mental apathy. He was found in a perilous state of indecision. But having put into practice the psychological teaching of the Gita, it is not long before he is found placed himself in a situation full of power, confidence and decision, although the circumstances and surroundings remained quite unchanged.

Maharishi points out that a close study of Lord Krishna's discourse reveals a great depth of psychological insight. It also demonstrates that the individual mind however intelligent it may be on the superficial conscious level, can be easily overcome by its failure to comprehend a perplexing situation, which is obviously beyond its control, unless it is in tune with the unlimited cosmic mind that it can naturally decide and act in a situation, free from the contradictions and influences of the surroundings, and in consonance with the cosmic purpose of evolution.

The Gita declares in unambiguous terms, that the establishment of conscious co-ordination between the individual and the cosmic mind is the only sure way, to ensure that the individual becomes entirely free of the possibility of failing to understand a baffling situation and come out successfully, rising above its adverse effect.

The psychology of the Bhagavad-Gita, Maharishi points out, presents a master technique for bringing out this co-ordination of the individual mind with the cosmic mind, by bringing the attention of the mind to the field of the transcendental absolute existence. Thereby, the weakness and limitations of the individual mind are transformed into the unbounded strength of the cosmic intelligence.

It is pointed out that this great achievement is simple to achieve. Any and every individual on earth can easily succeed in it. In this way every individual can make it unnecessary to undergo all the complexities and innumerable sufferings in life.

This technique of Transcendental Meditation is the golden key to the wisdom of psychology, the study of the mind. The key is of practical value. It is a scientific method that could satisfy any intellect. It marks the fulfillment of modern psychology. This technique opens the way to absolute wisdom, supplementing and enriching all fields of relative existence and makes a man not only free from tension, but puts his mind in conformity with the cosmic mind, in tune with the cosmic purpose of evolution.

Fulfillment of Philosophy:

Fulfillment of philosophy has for its objective in making a man realize that the transitory values of day-to-day life co-exist with the permanent and imperishable values of eternal life.

Maharishi lays before the student of philosophy the following goals:

1.   The student of philosophy should know the reality of the established truth of life free from doubts regarding anything in the field of creation.

2.   He should not only be the knower of reality but, should directly experience the ultimate reality of life himself. He should actually live reality in life along with fully integrated values of life.

3.   He should be an eternally contented man living in divine consciousness. He should live a life of fulfillment.

4.   He should be the master of the art of living. He should be the knower of the science of Being.

Speaking about what the modern study of philosophy does to students of philosophy, Maharishi says, it is pitiable. He says, philosophy has failed to reveal the truth to the people's of the world. Without dwelling on the failure of philosophy for the past centuries, Maharishi concerns himself to the field of fulfillment of philosophy and tries to explore and bring to the level of the common intelligence, the great values of the study of philosophy on the day-to-day practical life.

He therefore puts before the world his technique of Transcendental Meditation which enables an individual to explore the unseen regions and the ultimate reality of life. He therefore makes available to everyone on the level of one's own experience, the nature of the transcendental Being. The practice of Transcendental Meditation makes it possible for the conscious mind to come within the range of the field of transcendental Being and actually experience it.

The absolute Being as explained previously is the ultimate of creation. It is the ultimate reality. It is the truth of life. By truth, is meant that which never changes. Transcendental absolute Being is eternal in its nature; it remains the same. It is the ultimate constituent of creation which never changes, for, change belongs to the relative field of existence. Though it never changes and remains as absolute Being, it gives rise to the ever-changing diversity and multiplicity of forms and phenomena in creation.

The experience of absolute Being, gained during Transcendental Meditation leaves no doubt about the essential constituent of the entire structure of creation. During Transcendental Meditation, the mind dives deep within, and passes through the different strata of creation and ultimately arrives at transcendental Being. Between the gross strata of consciousness on the level of the ordinary conscious mind, and the transcendental consciousness of pure Being, lie all the different strata of creation.

In the practice of Transcendental Meditation not only the inner field of consciousness is unfolded, but the mind passes through the entire field of subtle creation. When the mind thus unfolds and activates the deeper levels of consciousness, it transcends all these strata of creation. This is how the mind gains more and more ability to cognise the entire universe. On this aspect Maharishi observes "All these inner mechanisms of the entire creation come to the conscious experience of the mind only by the practice of Transcendental Meditation. The practice unfolds the mysteries of nature and reveals to man the truth of creation and the entire field of life. Nothing remains hidden, everything becomes clear to the mind on the way to the transcendental state of pure consciousness". (Page 266- Science of Being and Art of Living-T.M.)

Maharishi further observes that the age-old quest for the experience of reality is fulfilled and the seekers of Truth and philosophers find their fulfillment in this simple system of Transcendental Meditation. The inner realms of life are unfolded. The essential nature of the ultimate reality is cognized. Everyone is thus able to know for himself the truth of creation, by his first-hand and personal experience and by a systematic understanding of it.

Herein lies the fulfillment of philosophy, which brings reality to a clear understanding on the intellectual level and at the same time brings reality to the positive, direct and personal experience.

Maharishi refers to the great expressions of the Vedic wisdom found in the Upanishads, which declare, unequivocally the oneness of life in such expressions as "I am That", "That Thou art", "Consciousness is Brahman", "This Self is Brahman", and says that they remain merely a fanciful imagination or at best, an intellectual mood, without the actual cognition of the ultimate absolute Being. The study of philosophy leaves man in the uncertainly of the nature of the supreme reality, without the direct experience of the transcendental Being. Maharishi, expresses that it is only the direct experience of the reality that succeeds, in eliminating the confusion by the different schools of philosophy.

In summing up his chapter on fulfillment of philosophy he offers his devotion and thanks to the great glory of His Divinity Swami Brahmananda Saraswati, Bhagavan Shankaracharya, the devotion to whom has revealed to him the key to the fulfillment of philosophy. He says it is only by such revelation that the path of the seekers of Truth has been made easy of accomplishment, and the goal has been achieved. He observes that the path lies in learning the techniques of Transcendental Meditation and practicing it everyday and arriving at the goal many times, during the daily practice. He refers to this as the fulfillment of philosophy.

PART V

Paths to God realization:

God:

It is said that the conception of God, is a reality greater than the reality of any conception that the human mind has ever developed at anytime. It is not a fanciful thought, a thought to hide, or a thought to serve as a shelter or refuge. God is a reality more concrete than any of the realities of the entire cosmos. The existence of God is more permanent, and more substantial than the ever changing temporary existence of the forms and phenomena of creation.

God is found in two phases of the reality: one phase of the reality is the supreme Being of absolute eternal nature. The other phase of the reality is the personal God at the top of the phenomenal creation. Thus God has two aspects, the personal and the impersonal. They are the two realities of the word God.

Impersonal aspect of God:

The impersonal aspect of God is formless and supreme. It is eternal and absolute. It is without attributes, qualities or features, because these pertain only to the relative field of life and creation. The impersonal God is of absolute nature beyond all relative phenomenal existence.

But all the attributes of relative creation have their basis in the attribute-less absolute Being of impersonal and of unmanifested nature.

By its very nature, the impersonal absolute God is progressive. Even though, it appears manifested in different degrees and forms. It maintains it's status as the unmanifested absolute.

So it can be said, that the impersonal Omnipresent God, remaining always impersonal and omnipresent, appears in the relative field in the form of creation, guided by its own nature.

Maharishi illustrates this by taking the example of hydrogen and oxygen. Remaining as hydrogen and oxygen the substance takes on different qualities and appears as vapour, water and ice. Similarly, omnipresent impersonal almighty Being, while remaining as the absolute omnipresent Being, manifests into different qualities of forms and phenomena in creation. The impersonal absolute God is the ultimate reality of life. It is life eternal. It knows no change in its character. It is the ultimate of creation. It is the power of the omnipresent impersonal God, that keeps the world in its existence in the past, present and feature. Just as there is only one essential constituent H_2O, in vapour, water and ice, the ultimate essential constituent of the entire creation, the impersonal absolute God is one. But it appears as many in creation. The appearance of the one as many is only phenomenal. The reality of the one impersonal God is still eternal and absolute.

In the never-changing eternal absolute Being, are founded all the ever-changing forms and phenomena of the relative existence. The never-changing eternal absolute Being is the creator, maintainer and sustainer of the entire world of creation. It is called the creator because it is the basis of all creation; all creation comes out of it. To create is it's nature, to be is it's nature, to expand is it's nature. So, creating, being, and expanding are the different aspects of the nature of the almighty impersonal God. It is called the maintainer of creation, in the sense that it forms the essential constituent of creation. It is the sustainer in the sense, that all creation dwells in it. The world is sustained by it, and eventually dissolves into it.

To understand how the world dissolves into it's source, Maharishi explains, by taking the example of hydrogen and oxygen which take the different forms of vapour, water and ice. Just as the qualities of vapour dissolve into oxygen and hydrogen, their essential constituents, the qualities of water dissolve into their essential constituents, oxygen and hydrogen, so also, all the forms and phenomena of relative existence dissolved into their essential constituent Being, the impersonal absolute eternal God, the almighty.

When we say that the absolute is almighty it is not in the sense that it is able to do everything. This is because being everything, it cannot do anything, and cannot know anything. Therefore it is beyond doing and knowing. It is almighty in the sense that without in nothing would be. All that exists is contained in its absolute status of Being. In this sense the impersonal God, is creator, maintainer and sustainer of the world, remaining eternally, in its unmanifested states, and only world, remaining eternally, in its unmanifested states, and only in that sense, it is almighty.

It has been previously stated that prana is the vibratory nature of Being, which transforms the unmanifested ocean of Being, into the manifested life stream of individual beings. So it is Being, pure consciousness, the impersonal almighty God, that appears both as the subject and the object.

We have previously pointed out that the individual seed of life is the unfulfilled karma of the past life of man. The sum total of all the unfulfilled desires of the past life of man acts as the seed of the individual, that shapes vibrating Being into the specific life stream of an individual. So the prana in conjunction with the desire forms the mind, and prana devoid of its association with the mind forms matter. This is how the subjective and objective aspects of the individual life come into existence. Essentially it is Being, which expresses itself as different aspects of the individual. Just as it is the seed which shapes the pattern of sap into a tree, in an individual's life it is the impression of the experiences of the past life that shapes Being into a specific pattern of individual life force, or prana.

The impersonal absolute Being, or God, is of transcendental nature beyond everything of relative existence. It is beyond belief, thought, faith, dogma and ritual. It lies beyond the field of understanding, beyond mind and intellect. It is beyond contemplation and intellectual discrimination and decisions. It is the state of Being. The Being of all is the omnipresent, impersonal God.

Because it is the Being of all, to realize it means just to be, what one already is. Being is realization of the impersonal, omnipresent God. Being is the essential oneself. Being can never be different from what one already is. So, in order to be oneself it is only necessary to come out of the personal nature, come out of the relative field of doing and thinking and be established in the field of Being. Being is therefore the realization of the impersonal.

It has been shown while dealing with Transcendental Meditation, that it is only necessary to gain the habit of arriving at Being, by coming out of the gross into the subtle levels of thinking, and eventually transcending the subtlest.

Thus it is clear that the realization of the impersonal absolute God, is merely arriving at one's own Being. This shows that there exists no path between the experiencer and the impersonal. What exists is the eternal existence of the omnipresent impersonal Being. The impersonal is permeating the entire field of creation, as butter permeates the milk, or as oil permeates the seed. A practical way to reach the level of the oil in the seed is to enter into the subtle strata of the seed and reach the field of the oil. In a similar manner to reach the level of the butter in milk, it is necessary to enter into the subtle strata of a particle of milk, and reach the field of butter.

Therefore, the only way to realize the almighty impersonal God is to enter into the subtle strata of things, and then to transcend the subtlest experience. There will be found, the field of impersonal, the field of pure Being, the state of pure consciousness. This state of pure consciousness lies in the transcendental field of everything. Transcendental Meditation is transcendental absolute Being, the almighty transcendental God.

Maharishi points out that the word God has remained for the most part a fanciful, pleasant thought and a refuge, during suffering and misery in life. The custodians of many strange religions have used the word God, as a magic word to control the understanding and religious destiny of many an innocent soul. God, the omnipresent, is presented as something to fear. But God is not the power of fear; it is not something from which fear could emanate. God is the existence of bliss consciousness of absolute and eternal life. But there are religions existing in the world based on fear, and this fear is instilled in the children of God. Maharishi calls it cruel and detrimental to life, to spread fear in the name of God. God, is life eternal, purity and basis. The kingdom of God is the field of all good for man. God is to be realized, not to be feared.

The impersonal God is that Being which dwells in the heart of everyone. It is within one's self. Every individual in his true nature is the impersonal God. That is why, the vedic philosophy of the Upanishads declares: "I am that, Thou art That, and all this is that". One need not be afraid of his own self. No one need be afraid of the result of bliss. No one need be afraid of the kingdom of heaven, where there is only bliss and fulfillment.

The God almighty, the impersonal unmanifested Being, is the eternal reality of life. It is imperishable. It is abundance. It is life. It is fulfillment. It is within the reach of everyone to realize it. To reach it one has only to be it. The technique lies in the systematic practice of Transcendental Meditation.

Personal aspect of God:

Maharishi describes God in personal form as the supreme Being of almighty nature. It is called "Saguna Brahma" or "Mayashakti". It is he or she God. Some say it is both he and she. But it is not it, because of the personal character. It, as we have seen, belongs to the impersonal and transcendental aspect of God.

The personal aspect of God necessarily has form, qualities, features, likes and dislikes. It has the ability to command the entire existence of the cosmos, the process of evolution and all that there is in creation.

It is seen that there are grades in creation. Some forms, some beings, are less powerful, less intelligent, less creative, less joyful. Others have greater degrees of these attributes. The whole creation consists of different strata of intelligence, peace and energy.

We find that, at the lowest end of evolution, there exists the inert states of creation. From there the life of the species begins, and the creation changes in its intelligence, power and joyfulness. The progressive scale of evolution is carried on through the different species of vegetables, the egg-born, the water-born, the animal kingdom and rises to the world of angels. Ultimately on the top level of evolution, is he who has unlimited powers, joy, intelligence and energy. He is all knowing, all powerful and blissful. He is almighty and dwells at the top level of creation.

Maharishi explains, what is meant by saying that he possesses an almighty nature. He has the power to do, to be and to understand everything. As the supreme personal being placed at the top level of creation he possesses a nervous system, so highly developed, that his ability on every level of life would be unlimited. He would possess the most powerful senses and the most powerful mind. His intellect would be the most powerful intellect. He would possess the most powerful ego.

Such a statement about the supreme almighty God, presiding over the top level of creation does not seem illogical, especially when we observe the different levels of evolution in the fields of life below the species of man down to the inert creation. In this order of creation, we can also intellectually conceive of some stratum of evolution on the highest level of creation, where the life will be perfect, mind is perfect, and the intellect, ego and personality reach their levels of perfection. Between this highest state of evolution, where life has reached its perfection and the lowest state of evolution, where life begins to be, lies the whole range of creation.

So, this supreme almighty God, is as though controlling the entire creation. All the laws of nature are controlled by his will. He has set the whole field of evolution in an automatic manner. He is in complete harmony and conformity with all the laws of creation. With the dissolution of creation, the almighty personal God on top, also merges into the impersonal absolute state of the supreme. With the commencement of creation he comes back again to dwell on the highest stratum of creation. This is how the personal God, along with the whole of creation, keeps on eternally maintaining the cycle of creation, evolution and dissolution.

In this way the whole field of relative existence is governed by the laws of nature which automatically function in a perfect rhythm of life. That rhythm, that harmony of life, is maintained by the almighty will of the almighty God at the highest level of creation, who controls and commands the entire process of life. We can therefore understand intellectually the possibility of the existence of some supreme Being, in the form of a personal almighty God at the highest level of creation.

To get a clear conception of the almighty nature of personal God, we have to make it clear that almighty nature lies in the perfection of the senses, the mind, the intellect and ego. What could such a perfection mean in actual existence? When we say perfection, we mean, that if he has eyes he would be able to see all things at one time. If he has a nose, the almighty nose would be able to smell all the varieties of smells at one time. His ears would enable him to hear all the sounds of the entire cosmos at one time. His almighty mind would naturally be aware of anything, of any grade, at any time. His almighty intellect would comprehend and decide everything at any time. All the innumerable decisions that are the results of natural laws in the process of evolution, are the innumerable decisions of the almighty personal supreme God at the head of creation. He governs and maintains the entire field of evolution and the different lives of innumerable beings in the whole cosmos.

Maharishi points out that we can thus intellectually understand and arrive at the possibility of such an almighty supreme Being dwelling as the head of creation. If we can conceive of this, we should also be able to intellectually understand that, if we could somehow establish communion with that almighty supreme power, then our lives would be greatly benefited by the blessings of such a communion. We can also understand that the almighty supreme power whether he or she, is a personal Being and would have a particular nature of his of her own. The way to achieve his or her blessings would be to get the individual life in tune with his or her nature, and such an attempt would improve life at any level of creation. This would hasten the progress of evolution, and enable an individual life to arrive at the highest evolution as soon as possible. If the individual could mould his thought, speech and action in accordance with the nature of the supreme God, and succeed in tuning himself with him, or her, then, certainly the unevolved insignificant life of the individual will be blessed with the all-powerful, all-merciful nature of the almighty supreme God. Thus any main could gain the height of evolution.

Maharishi calls it the result of only poor understanding, if one could not intellectually conceive of the existence of the supreme almighty personal God. Anyone who could see the inert or the most unevolved creation at one end of existence, and see also the different rising grades of creation, should be able to intellectually conceive of the existence, and having done so, could aspire to the great realization.

It is understandable, says Maharishi, that one may not be able to appreciate the conception of personal God, or realize the personal God. But, he calls it the result of an undeveloped state of mind, if one were to refute the existence of the personal God.

He refers to God in the following terms, "God is the holiest of holy words, because, it brings to consciousness the supreme state of existence, the almighty status of the supreme Being. God realization has been said to be the aim of life". (page 275- Science of Being and Art of Living-T.M.).

It is said that an individual at any level of evolution will have God realization as his ultimate goal, because, when he is in tune with the almighty supreme Being, that will be the state of fulfillment, abundance, unlimited energy, creativity, intelligence and bliss.

Difference ways of God realization, the personal and impersonal God:

The two aspects of God are 1) impersonal omnipresent absolute Being and 2) personal supreme Being. The realization of God could mean the realization of the impersonal God or the realization of the personal God. The realization of the impersonal God will naturally be on the transcendental level of consciousness. Anything in the relative field cannot be omnipresent; relative means bound by time, space and causation.

The plane of the omnipresent is unbounded by time, space and causation. The realization of the personal God will be on the level of human perception. It will be on the level of the sensory experience. It involves, that the eyes should see the supreme person. The heart should be able to feel the qualities of the supreme person. The realization of the personal God has to be in the relative field of life. Thus the realization of the impersonal God is in transcendental consciousness of the waking state.

We have already seen, that the nature of the impersonal God is absolute bliss consciousness of transcendental nature. To realize it, the conscious mind should transcend all the limits of experience in the relative field and should enter into the field beyond relative existence, where the conscious mind would be left to remain conscious all by itself. For this to happen the conscious mind has to be brought from the present level of experience, to the subtler levels of experience and eventually to transcend the subtlest level of experience, and consciously arrive at the transcendental field of existence.

Maharishi then examines the possible ways of bringing the conscious mind to the field of transcendental Being.

It is seen that the body, or the nervous system is the principal mechanism, responsible for the abstract mind to have an experience. For any experience to happen, it is necessary for the nervous system to adjust itself to certain specific conditions. The knowledge of the working of the nervous system reveals to us, that for a person to see something, a particular part of the brain has to function in a particular manner. Similarly, when a person hears, thinks or smells, for each activity, different parts of the brain come to function. So, depending on the activity of the mind, a corresponding activity will be set up in the nervous system. Hence to produce a particular experience in the mind, it is necessary to bring the nervous system to a state of specific activity.

If the mind is thinking about an object, the thought of the object could be experienced, only when the specific part of the brain begins to function in a particular manner. From this, we can conclude that the thought of the object could be experienced in two ways. In the first case, the mind starts the process of thinking, and correspondingly stimulates the nervous system, and this process of thinking goes on stimulating the nervous system, until the particular portion of the brain attains to that level of activity, which makes it possible for the mind to experience the thought of the object, or, alternatively, if such an activity in the brain could be produced physiologically, then also, the mind would experience the thought of the object. Hence an experience could be had in two ways.

1. Either, the mind starts the process of thinking and goes on stimulating the nervous system for the particular experience, or,

2. The nervous system is stimulated in a particular fashion which creates an activity, making it possible for the mind, to experience the desired object.

Maharishi further observes, that the realization of the transcendental Being is an experience, and hence, the realization of the impersonal God means positive experience of the transcendental reality of life. This, being an experience necessitates bringing the nervous system to a specific state of activity or conditioning.

If it is possible that this activity, or conditioning of the nervous system, could be attained by physiological means, then, that would constitute the physiological approach to the realization of the impersonal God.

Having thus arrived at the path to God realization from the physiological consideration, we can categories the path to realization of the impersonal God, under five different groups:

1. Psychological or intellectual approach.
2. Emotional approach.
3. Physiological approach.

4.   Mechanical approach.

5.   Psycho-Physiological approach.

Of the above five paths to God realization, the intellectual approach to God realization would be suitable for those, who are cultured intellectually, and who have reached a high degree of intellectual attainment.

The emotional approach to God realization is suitable for those, whose qualities of heart are in a highly developed state, and show qualities of love and devotion.

Those who are cultured neither emotionally, nor intellectually, can adopt the other two approaches to realization, namely physiological and mechanical.

The physiological approach to God realization involves bringing the body and nervous system to a specific state, which enables the mind to be established on a level of consciousness of the transcendental nature of existence. The physiological method is suitable for those people who are physiologically normal, and whose nervous system is functioning as near normal as possible. Whatever may be their intellectual or emotional culture, if their nervous system is normal, the physiological approach would raise their level of consciousness. Maharishi observes that, in order to produce a particular state of the nervous system, without the training of the mind of heart would require a great amount of sustained physical or physiological training.

The psycho-physiological approach is a way, which can be used by the people, who want to approach the problem of God from both ends, physical and mental. This involves the training of the mind and body simultaneously.

The mechanical path however, is suited to any man however weak his mind, heart and nervous system might be.

We shall deal briefly, with these different paths as described by Maharishi.

Intellectual path to God realization:

We have previously seen that the transcendental omnipresent Being, being of omnipresent nature is the essential Being of everyone. It forms the basic life of one and all, and is one's own Self or Being. By intellectual path we only mean that it is a way of realizing one's own self. It is the direct experience of the essential nature of our own self, or transcendental Being.

The intellectual path to God realization is the path of knowledge (Jnana Marga). In this path, the vehicle which enables a man to advance on the path of knowledge is discrimination, or, the power of intellect or the power of analysis. In this method, only the intellect functions. Here the qualities of the heart, the path of mechanical perception, and physiological means have no place. Here everything is scrutinized and analysed and understood through discrimination based on reason and logic. Nothing is accepted except on the basis of logic and precision. The intellect has to be wide awake. It is a very delicate path to realization.

Here the nature of the world and reality are taught from a teacher, who has himself come to the cognition of the divine nature through the path of intellectual discrimination. Maharishi points out that certain essential steps are necessary in this path. The aspirant hears from the realized soul about the nature of conclusions arrived at by him. He hears from him,

1.   that creation is perishable.
2.   that everything in this world is changing and relative,
3.   that time-space-causation-bound manifested creation of forms and phenomena forms the perishable aspect of life

Having been taught about this by the realized soul, the aspirant begins to distinguish between one state from the other, and eventually comes to the conclusion about the fact of the futile, and impermanent nature of creation (Anitya).

The discrimination between the different phases of life leads him to the conclusion, that the whole field of life is a field of ever changing and of perishable nature. This is the first lesson on the intellectual path of enlightenment. After careful analysis he comes to the conclusion that the world is not real, even though it seems to be, that these things of the world are always changing, and that which is always changing, has no real and everlasting status of its own.

But on the level of the senses however, the world seems to be real. But through the intellect we decide that, because the world is ever-changing it cannot be real. The real is described as that, which will always remain the same. But at the same time, the world cannot be dismissed as unreal, because we do experience it.

Maharishi makes this clear, by taking the example of a tree. The tree is there because we experience it. We cannot say, that the tree is not there. If we say that the tree is unreal, we will have to say that it does not exist. But that is not the case and we are not in a position to make such a statement. We acknowledge that the tree is there. But at the same time, we must also say that it is always changing. Because it is always changing, it is not real, but, because it is there for all practical purposes, we have to credit the tree with the status of existence.

What is that status between the real and unreal? Maharishi calls it "Phenomenal existence". The phenomenon of the tree is there, even though it is not real. So the tree has a "phenomenal" reality. In Sanskrit it is called 'mithya'.

Thus, the aspirant begins to discriminate between the temporary values of the world, and his quest for finding something permanent. This sense of discrimination eventually reveals to him the perishable nature of the entire creation. As the aspirant contemplates on the perishable nature of creation, the quest for finding something deeper, takes his mind to some the quest for finding something deeper, takes his mind to some deeper reality underlying the ever-changing phase of existence.

When the aspirant gains some insight into the reality of inner life, he is able to contemplate the abstract metaphysical reality of imperishable nature, and to realize the hidden secrets of existence, that lie beyond the ever-changing phenomenal phase of life.

To distinguish between the phenomenal and the real Maharishi gives the example of the tree.

In a tree the aspirant finds its different forms the trunk, branches, flowers and fruit. He finds that the tree changes everyday, new leaves springing, old leaves drying, branches failing and new branches growing. Thus the whole existence of the tree is set up in an ever-changing pattern. But behind all these ever-changing phenomenal phases of the tree, he finds something that doest not change, and remains the same all the time. The nourishment or sap drawn from the root remains the same all the time. It is the sap, which appears in the different forms of branches, leaves, flowers and fruits. The different aspects of the tree change, but the sap remains unchanged all the time. The transformation of the sap into the different aspects of the tree reveals the hidden mystery of nature.

The aspirant finds, that, behind the ever-changing phases of phenomenal existence, there exists some reality of an unchangeable nature. There exists some phase of existence, which is never changing, but, which gives rise to all the changeable aspects of phenomenal creation.

When the power of discrimination reveals to the aspirant, the possibility of the existence of some never-changing reality at the basis of the ever-changing phenomenal creation, the aspirant enters into the second phase of the path of knowledge. He begins to contemplate upon the never-changing permanent phase of life, the unchanging aspect of existence, which is the reality of life.

When he has thoroughly assimilated the idea of the impermanence of creation, and the phenomenal nature of creation, and when his intellect has been firmly established in the idea, then he begins to dwell on the permanent never-changing sphere of life. Like the example of sap in the tree, analogies in the material world of creation, distinguishing between the phenomenal and the real, help the aspirant to discover the meta-physical truth, lying beyond the phenomenal phase of existence.

Contemplation on the inner value of life eventually reveals to the aspirant, that the ever-changing world of phenomena is based on a never-changing element of no-form and no-phenomenon. He finds that all forms and phenomena belong to the relative field of existence, whereas, that, which lies beyond all forms and phenomena, belongs to a field that is out of relativity.

This is how the seeker of God, treading the intellectual path to enlightenment, finds his mind firmly established in the impermanence of creation, and on the permanence of the transcendental reality of life. Now what remains is to realize it.

As the practice of contemplation continues, his mind begins to be established, more and more in eternal Being, as his own self. He begins to contemplate in terms of "I am That", "Thou art That", "All this is That". The idea of the oneness of life becomes so deeply rooted in his consciousness, that, with prolonged practice of contemplation, he begins to live this understanding through the vicissitudes of daily life.

Having gained the oneness of life, the aspirant begins to hold his mind in the oneness of existence steadfastly, amidst all the relative phenomenal experiences and actions in his daily life. His consciousness is enchanted by the idea of oneness of life, and the apparent diversity of existence and phenomenal creation begins to lose its hold on him. This is the beginning of the experience of the transcendental reality on the level of intellectual understanding.

The next step is to ponder over, assimilate, and establish that oneness of eternal life in terms of one's own Being. This is done through the practice of establishing in the depth of consciousness the oneness of eternal life, by contemplating in terms of, I am that, thou art that, and all this is that.

Maharishi describes the path of enlightenment as a path of self-hypnotism. He makes a distinction between the intellectual side of enlightenment and the state of actual realization. He observes that discrimination of the ever-changing phenomenal existence, and the attempt to locate an unchanging underlying reality is one thing, and the identification of one's own Being with the Being of the entire creation is another. Maharishi further points out that, unless the understanding of the oneness of life goes deep in one's consciousness, and begins to be lived, in the midst of all the diverse experiences and activity of every day life, it will not be a state of realization. Therefore the aspirant on the intellectual path of realization has not only to understand, and assimilate the idea of the oneness of Being, but also try to live the unchanging, imperishable oneness of absolute Being, in terms of his own Being.

With continued contemplation the idea of the oneness of life goes so deep into the aspirant's consciousness, that the experiences of his mind, in the wakeful, dreaming and deep sleep states, do not in any way weaken his conviction that he is the imperishable unchanging eternal absolute Being.

When this conviction become firmly rooted in the consciousness of the aspirant he begins to live that oneness of life through all the diverse fields of life, in the wakeful, dreaming and deep sleep states. When he rises to the state of eternal Being, while yet, he remains in the relative field of experience, then his consciousness is complete and becomes cosmic consciousness and his life is fully realized.

This is the realization of the omnipresent impersonal God through the intellectual path of God realization.

Maharishi points out certain disadvantage that exist in the pursuit of this path of enlightenment. They are:

1. The nature of this path is such that it cultivates in the mind of the aspirant a sense of loss of interest in his practical life and day-to-day activity.

2. Since the mind is of contemplative nature, the mind first begins to think in terms of negation of creation, its futility, and the impermanence of the perishable nature of the phenomenal existence of the world.

3. Secondly it contemplates on the imperishable nature that lies as a deeper reality of life behind the obvious phase of life.

4. the mind begins to always think, contemplate, and try to assimilate the transcendental reality in contrast to the perishable phenomenal existence and tries to live to reality. Hence it begins to lose the charm of the life of the outside world.

5. such a mind necessarily becomes detached, useless and hopeless for all practical purposes in life. Therefore, certainly, the intellectual path of God realization is not suited for practical men. Maharishi puts it, that this path is not suited for the householder. No man remaining in the world and shouldering the responsibility of family and society, and the pressure of business can possibly ever succeed in this path, in infusing the divine nature into his mind. Being the method of contemplation this path of intellectual revelation is suitable only for such people who have forsaken the world, and who have chosen the way of a recluse, and who have kept themselves away from the responsibilities of life and society. The way of a recluse keeps him silent, contemplative and discrimination most of the time, assimilating the divine nature as his own. The success in this path of contemplation involves a long time devotion to this path, before the aspirant achieves any degree of success. Anyway, this is not the path of a house holder, because, a householder has to discharge great responsibilities in his life, and this path of negation and abstinence in work, makes him an irresponsible man in the world.

The practice of 'Rajayoga' also belongs to this type of intellectual approach to God realization, and is similarly accomplished through contemplation and concentration, and is not suitable for a householder. For a householder, it is only a path through action and not through contemplation, that is required. The intellectual approach to God realization along with the behaviour in the world, disturbs the co-ordination of the body and mind, and brings disharmony in the life of the aspirant. It prevents the possibility of any development of higher consciousness.

Maharishi at this point, observes that many seekers of enlightenment for centuries past, who have taken to this path have been the victims of this state, which has resulted in their failure in the world, and also failure in the divine quest as well. True enlightenment through the intellectual path involves raising the consciousness above the field of the intellect, and arriving at the field of the transcendental divine consciousness. This will mean bringing the conscious mind to the level of the transcendental reality. Short of realizing the above state, any intellectual mood making of any type, does not help much and succeed in bringing the aspirant to the state of God realization.

Emotional path to God realization, path of devotion or Bhakti Marga:

The path of devotion or Bhakti Marga involves the qualities of heart. All the paths of devotion are emotional paths to God realization. The qualities of the heart are the qualities that enable a man to feel. They differ from the qualities of the mind which involve the intellect and enable a man to know and understand.

In the intellectual path to God realization man knows and understands, and discriminates. But in the path of devotion the main factor is feeling. It is the feeling of love which enables a man to advance on the path of devotion. The qualities of the heart that sustain the path of devotion are, the increasing capacity of love, emotion, happiness, kindness, devotion and surrender. On the path of devotion, as one advances, love increases and leaves behind fields of lesser happiness, and a devotee gains ground on more stable, more important and more valuable fields of happiness. The path of devotion is the path of happiness, the path of love and the path through the qualities of the heart.

Maharishi observes that love of God is the greatest virtue that a man could ever cultivate. Through love of God develops love for the creation of God, for the children of God. When love of God grows in the heart, kindness, compassion, tolerance and helpfulness to others flow. With respect to devotion and feeling of love for God, Maharishi observes "Fortunate are those whose life is dedicated to the almighty God, and to the doing of good to his creation. Increased devotion means increased love, and this amounts to increased happiness, contentment, glory and grace" (Page 284-Science of Being and Art of Living-T.M.).

On the path of devotion, one feels increasing degree of happiness as one proceeds further on this path. The path of love becomes the path of bliss. With the increase of love in the heart of the devotee, he gains a greater degree of happiness. His heart finds its goal when his love rests in the eternal existence of God. Then the devotee and God become one.

A man of devotion finds God in the world and the world is found in God. From devotion to God, happiness increases. On the surface of life happiness is limited. It is only when the attention is diverted to the inner fields of life, and to the subtler levels of creation, and to the deeper levels of consciousness, happiness increases and becomes lasting. Man begins to experience the deeper levels of happiness. Bringing the experience of greater happiness this is the method of Transcendental Meditation. Maharishi points out that the path of love and devotion without the practice of Transcendental Meditation, without experience of great happiness is not practical.

The practice of Transcendental Meditation, it is said, constantly increases the ability to experience greater happiness in the heart of the devotee, and thus enables him, to continue in the path of love and devotion until he feels the fullness of eternal bliss, and then the ocean of love becomes full to the brim. It makes the devotee experience absolute love, which becomes a real significant personal experience. The devotee finds himself founded in the impersonal eternal God consciousness and finds his fulfillment in the path of devotion and love.

Physiological approach to God realization:

Maharishi speaks of a physiological approach to God realization. He examines the question whether there could be a physiological means to God realization, and whether, it would be possible to rise to cosmic consciousness from the physical plane. His approach is entirely scientific, and enables us to aspire, to reach the pinnacle of human development from the physical side of life. He points out that the state of divine existence, or divine life, or God realization, is a state of positive experience. It is not a fanciful thought, neither is it an intellectual mood. The state of divine experience is not on the thinking level. It is an actual state of life, it is the state of Being, it is Being itself.

It has already been explained, that for an experience to happen, there has to be a specific activity created in the nervous system. The nervous system has to set itself in a particular manner, for the specific state of experience. To give rise to a very subtle state of thought, there has to be a correspondingly subtle activity in the subtle part of the nervous system. When the meditation transcends the subtlest thought, and reaches the transcendental state, it will be a state of suspension, silence and full awareness of pure consciousness. In this state the experiencer is left all by himself, without any object of experience. It is a state of pure consciousness, a state of positive experience of pure Being. The experience of pure Being and the state of Being mean the same thing.

For this experience to take place the nervous system has to be in a particular type of set-up. It will be a state of poised or balanced alertness. In this state the nervous system is neither active not passive. It is active but has no activity, because there is no experience of any outside object. At the same time, the nervous system is not as completely passive as in deep sleep. Therefore, it can be said to be active without activity. It is passive without passivity. It is neither active nor passive. It is a state of restful alertness, as Maharishi calls this state.

During meditation at every level of the subtle experience of the word, or mantra, the brain functions at different levels of activity. Even so, in the state of the experience of the transcendental, there is a specific state of the brain mechanism, which gives rise to the experience of the transcendental consciousness. The brain comes to state of suspension, of activity and no activity. But this is not the common state of the brain. It doest not take place during waking, dreaming or deep sleep states.

One way to bring about the set up of the brain for the state of the transcendental, is to experience the subtle states of thought until the subtlest state is experienced and transcended. By this process, the set-up of the brain required to give rise to the experience of the transcendental consciousness is brought about, step by step, through the process of experience. It is brought about through the agency of the mind. This is the mental approach to God realization.

Maharishi argues, that it should therefore be possible to create physically, a particular state of the nervous system, which will correspond to the state of the nervous system, giving rise to the experience of the transcendental consciousness. We find that, when the nervous system is tired, a state is created in which the brain doest not experience anything. In a similar manner by stimulating the nervous system physiologically, it should be possible to create a particular state of the nervous system which gives the brain mechanism, the particular set-up required for enabling the mind to experience the transcendental consciousness.

If this is physiologically possible, this would constitute the physiological approach to God realization.

The "Hatha Yoga" which existed in ancient times in India is a path of enlightenment, in which the body is forcefully controlled to bring about forced control over breathing, in order to control the mind to cultivate God consciousness. It is a physiological approach to God realization whereby, the nervous system is brought to a state which gives rise to a particular set-up of brain functioning, which enables the mind to experience transcendental consciousness.

It has been previously seen, that in order to have the experience of transcendental consciousness, the activity of the brain has to cease, but the brain should not be allowed to be static. The brain is to be held in a state of no activity, and yet is not passive. It is awake, and alert in itself. If the brain has to be held in a state of suspension, then the entire nervous system has to be held in a particular state, in a state of neither activity, nor inactivity. In order that this may happen, the breath has to be held in a state of neither breathing out, nor, breathing in. the breath has to be between flowing and not flowing, but, it has to be there.

In order to bring the body to that state of suspension the body has to be trained, because, the habit of the body is to be either in activity in the waking state, or, to be static in the sleeping state. This is the ordinary condition of the body. It must therefore be trained to be still, but yet, not to go into a passive state. This is done by controlling the body and breath, whereby, the nervous system is brought to a state, which gives, the particular set-up of the brain mechanism, to establish the mind in the state of transcendental consciousness.

When the body is normally functioning the general experience is that we are either awake or asleep. When we are about to go to sleep, we are aware to some extent when sleep comes, by the gradual dullness which overtakes us. The ability to experience becomes less and less, but, we do not know, when exactly sleep actually comes. We do feel, when we are about to sleep, and we do feel that our consciousness gradually becomes fainter, and then we do not feel anything. Consciousness fades to nil, but we are not aware of, and do not experience the actual fading of consciousness. Maharishi points out, that this shows that the body, or the mind, is not purely normal. If the whole nervous system were just normal, then, it should be possible for us to experience the subtlest state of awareness, the state of awareness which is almost one with deep sleep, and at the same time, almost one with the subtlest state of the wakeful state.

It is seen that in the ordinary state of the mind, when a thought arises, it overshadows the mind and then the brain is engaged in that thought. When the thought is translated into action, the purpose of the thought is achieved and the desire is fulfilled.

If the brain is functioning normally, once the desire is fulfilled, and before another desire arises, the mind will experience the state of pure Being, or pure consciousness. This is what happens in the case of a realized man. When he has a desire his mind is functioning, but when the desire is fulfilled and before another desire arises, he enjoys the natural state of Being. This is because, there is no activity in the brain. Being fee from activity, the brain does not go to a state of passivity. It cherishes the state of pure Being or pure consciousness. This happens in the case of a "Stithapragna".

It is seen that in between to thoughts, is the state of pure Being. Every thought arises from the state of pure Being and between two thoughts there is a gap. The gap should not be the gap of no experience. If the brain is functioning normally, if the mind is pure, if the nervous system is pure, then between every two thoughts, the state of pure Being will be experienced. But this is not generally the case.

The physiological approach is meant to improve the physical condition of the nervous system from being dull. Therefore it should aim in removing the impurity in the body, and also remove the reasons for fatigue. This is the physical approach, and also remove the reasons for fatigue. This is the physical approach. The purpose is, that the nervous system should be purified to such a great extent, that eventually, it will be able to create the exact set-up of the nervous system, which gives rise to the experience of transcendental consciousness. The physical condition of the nervous system should be so created as to cause the body to be in the most normal condition.

Maharishi points out that the make up of human nervous system is so evolved that it is perfect. The nervous system has the ability to experience the transcendental consciousness. But wrong food eaten, the wrong liquid consumed, and the impure air breathed, all make the nervous system to become unfit to give rise to the natural experience of the transcendental state. Hence the physiological approach to divine consciousness consists of the following essential requirements:

1, selecting proper quality of food, 2, Selecting the proper type of activity and 3. Eliminating from the system the influence of wrong food and wrong activity.

All these requirements naturally impose much discipline on all levels of life. Such an approach is only suitable to the hermit's way of life, where an aspirant can afford to spend time under the personal supervision of a teacher. But such an approach is certainly not suitable for the householder, whose pattern of life is such, that he cannot undergo the laborious and time consuming practices. Maharishi assures that one need not be disappointed on this account, because, there are other ways that are available to bring enlightenment, and which are more suitable to the busy householder of modern times.

Mechanical path to God realization:

Maharishi points out that a close scrutiny of the process of perception will reveal that God realization is possible in a mechanical way. Let us see, how maharishi has developed his thesis of perception.

Maharishi observes, that perception is the result of the natural radiation of consciousness from the center of pure Being in man on to the object to be perceived. It is not light from outside, which falls on the retina of the eye, that causes perception, although, light serves as one of the instruments for causing perception. The radiation of consciousness from the center of pure Being starts and through the nervous system reaches the senses of perception, and passes on to the object of experience. As it proceeds to radiate outward the content of consciousness, the degree of bliss diminishes. The whole process is automatic and mechanical. Maharishi observes. "The nervous system is the means through which consciousness manifests and projects itself to the outside world, resulting in the phenomenon of perception". (Page 293- Science of Being and art of Living-T.M.)

The process of perception is automatic and mechanical. If we want to see an object, we open the eyes and the sight of the object results automatically. This does not involve the use of the intellect or the emotions. This is what is meant by the statement that perception is a mechanical process.

The radiation of consciousness which starts from the abstract, absolute, pure state of Being, carries the bliss content in a diminishing degree, as it proceeds outward. Further, the oneness of Being which appears as many in its infinite variety in the relative creation, is an automatic projection of consciousness outward.

Perception in the outside world therefore results mechanically from the diverging process of consciousness. The degree of bliss decreases as we proceed to the outward gross levels of experience, and it increases as we move towards the subtler levels approaching the source of bliss. Being so, whether we experience on the levels of outward projecting consciousness, or, experience on different levels of inward-projecting consciousness, the process of perception remains mechanical and automatic. Hence Maharishi concludes, that perception remains automatic, whether it is the perception of the transcendental state of Being. This is how realization of Being is found on the mechanical plane of perception. This justifies the mechanical process of perception, as a means to God realization.

The process of perception in the outward direction results in the progressive increase of activity in the nervous system, whereas, the process of perception in the inward direction, is the result of diminishing activity of the nervous system. In the inward direction the process of perception is directed towards the one eternal existence, the oneness of the eternal life, the oneness of the nervous system, until the entire nervous system ceases to function and reaches a state of stillness, a state of restful alertness. Maharishi calls such a state which brings the realization of God, "Be still and know that I am God". (Page 294-Science of Being and Art of Living-T.M.)

In this state of stillness of mind, the activity of the nervous system is brought to a state of restful alertness. The activity of the mind is reduced to nil, and the thinking process has been reduced to a point at the source of thinking. At this point, perception remains in the state of absolute consciousness, marking the state of enlightenment, where, absolute Being of the transcendental nature comes to the conscious level of life. This is the mechanical path to God realization. In its practical form it is known as Transcendental Meditation. It is called a "Mechanical path" to God realization, because the process of inward perception doest not need any intellectual or emotional help. It doest not proceed through discrimination or feeling. The mechanical path of perception succeeds independently without intellectual or emotional interference.

In its inward direction, the mind reaches the field of transcendental absolute, and the mind in filled with the power of eternal Being. Then, when the mind returns to the outer world, it brings the light of transcendental absolute Being to bear on the outer world, thereby, increasing the intensity of bliss in the perception of the gross manifested world of creation. This would brighten all the fields of life in the world.

Speaking about this path of mechanical perception, Maharishi says, "This is how the innocent path of mechanical perception quietly serves to take the mind to transcendental absolute Being, or, to take the man to the field of God, and from there, bring him out with the glory of God to brighten all the fields of life in the world". (Page 295-Science of Being and Art of Living-T.M.)

Maharishi calls this as a path of action, and justifies its status as a path to enlightenment. In the Bhagavad-Gita this path is termed as the path of action or Karma Yoga. Maharishi claims that this path fills the whole field of life of the individual with the glory of divine Being, and brings individual life to the state of cosmic consciousness.

Any individual by following this path can realize God, irrespective of his intellectual or emotional state of development. One should only know how to use one's ability of experience or the mechanics of perception. This knowledge to make use of one's ability of perception opens the highway to God realization.

Maharishi observes that the mechanical path of God realization, as found in Transcendental Meditation, is so simple and comprehensive in its results, that it becomes alluring for all the lovers of God and seekers of truth, proceeding on any of the paths of God realization, whether the path is intellectual, emotional, physiological or psychological. The path supplements and reinforces any path to fulfillment.

Psycho-physiological approach:

The psycho-physiological approach involves the simultaneous use of the body and mind. The body and the mind are closely inter-related, as we have previously seen. The state of the mind directly affects the body and the state of the body influences the mind:

Under physiological approach to God realization, it has previously been stated that, by culturing the body and breath, the state of restful alertness could be created in the nervous system, so that the individual may have the experience of Being. This therefore leads us to infer that in any path of God realization, whether it is intellectual, or emotional, the pace of progress of God realization can be accelerated, by supplementing it with the features of the physiological approach.

The combination of the aspects of physiological path with the intellectual or emotional paths, constitutes the psycho-physiological path to God realization.

In this combined path to God realization the body and mind are cultured simultaneously, to produce the state of transcendental consciousness with regard to the mind, and the state of restful alertness with regard to the body. The purpose is to provide help from the physical plane to culture the mind, and from the mental plane for the culture of the body. This facilities arriving at the goal with greater ease and facility, in the least amount of time.

Lovers of God and seekers of Truth would be naturally attracted to follow the path of greater ease and comfort for the quick realization of God. But it has already been pointed out, that the physiological path requires rigorous practices of physical control and breath control, which is not suitable to the house-holder's way of life. Hence the scope of the psycho-physiological approach gets restricted from being universal. Further, culturing the body and breath, needs close personal supervision by a teacher, for safeguarding the health of the student. But there are some suitable light exercises for the body and breathing, which may be practiced simultaneously with the intellectual or emotional path, which do not require strict personal supervision. This would help to accelerate the progress towards God realization on these paths.

The psycho-physiological approach to God realization finds its fulfillment in the practice of Transcendental Meditation, which simultaneously influences the body and the mind. The practice of Transcendental Meditation, without any sort of control, on any level, automatically places the mind in the state of transcendental consciousness, and brings the body and the nervous system to that state of restful alertness which is most suited to the state of enlightenment.

Maharishi concludes by saying that the mental and the physical aspects of the psycho-physiological path are simultaneously fulfilled by the practice of Transcendental Meditation.

PART-VI

Generation after Generation:

Maharishi writes under this caption that every man in every generation is born a new man. He has a new ideal for fulfillment. He is born afresh. He has a new aspiration in life and new ideal to fulfill. It may be, that his aspirations coincide with the aspirations of the people around him, but for him they are afresh. They are his own aspirations for his fulfillment of life. Maharishi says, that a solid foundation for all men in all generations to gain fulfillment in life on all levels should be established and that responsibility for this, rests squarely on the shoulders of the great men of the present generation.

Maharishi then sets the goal of human fulfillment as below:

Every man needs sound physical and mental health. He should possess greater ability of action and greater capacity to think clearly. He should obtain greater efficiency in his work. He should be able to establish more loving, and more rewarding relationships with his fellow beings, and should be able to secure greater accomplishments in life on all levels. Man should obtain freedom from suffering and misfortune in day-to-day living. Towards the securing of the above results he should possess enough intelligence and vitality to satisfy the desires of his mind, along with contentment in his life. Along with these objectives, he should aim in living a life of permanent freedom in God consciousness.

It has been indicated previously under all the topics that have been dealt, that all the above qualities and virtues are gained by the regular and systematic practice of Transcendental Meditation and taking life easy and unstrained in the day-to-day routine.

Simplicity and purity of natural behaviour with other people, together with the regularity in the practice of Transcendental Meditation are claimed to accomplish all these qualities and virtues in the individual life of all people, of all generations for the present, and for the future.

In recommending a proper plan for the emancipation of the entire human race, generation after generation, Maharishi gives primary consideration for the factor of purity. He says, "Purity is life. Absolute purity is eternal life. Survival depends upon purity. The basis of the plan should be purity". (Page 298-Science of Being and Art of Living-T.M.)

Maharishi explains the factor of purity thus. In the state of cosmic consciousness, when the mind is brought to the fullest degree of infusion of absolute Being, the mind by nature, functions on the plane of purity. It is then in accordance with the natural laws of cosmic evolution, which carry out the process of evolution of everything in creation. He says, that any system or principle of life which could be based on the level of natural evolution in creation will certainly survive all the ages to come, because, it is the process of evolution which conducts the march of time through all the vicissitudes of life. The sole purpose of the plan, according to Maharishi, should aim at the continuity of the teaching of Transcendental Meditation, in the successive generation, and for this to be attained, a system has to be evolved which is based on the natural laws of evolution.

In view of the above considerations, Maharishi enunciates the following as the requirements of the plan, which are summarized below. They are relevant for all times to come and in all countries.

1. To see that the teaching of Transcendental Meditation is imparted on the level of the natural laws governing the process of evolution, the teachers who impart this knowledge should themselves be established on the plane of the cosmic law or at least, must strive sincerely towards this end in their own lives.

2. The teachers must be trained thoroughly in the practice and in the theoretical understanding of Transcendental Meditation.

3. Academies of meditation for training of teachers under ideal conditions for meditation are to be established in all the continents of the world.

4. To see that the teaching is imparted on the level of the natural process of evolution of the individual, it is necessary, that the teaching takes into consideration the natural tendency of the individuals. Nothing should be done to disturb their natural inclinations, because, that represents their paths of

evolution. They should be allowed to follow their paths of evolution, to be what they are, to do what they like, and not to do what they do not like.

5. The teaching of Transcendental Meditation should be such, as to bring to every individual the fulfillment of his desires, tendencies and inclinations and ways of life, through the practice of Transcendental Meditation. It is only then, that it will not only be readily accepted by the people, but, would certainly improve them and accelerate their progress on the path of their evolution.

6. the technique of imparting Transcendental Meditation should find out the aspirations in the life of the individuals, what they want to accomplish, and what their desires are. It should appraise them of the gains that accrue, by the practice of Transcendental Meditation in terms of their desires, needs and aspirations in life. It is only then, that the whole stream of their lives will be set in tune with the level of their lives will be set in tune with the level of their evolution, and will regulate their lives in accordance with the natural laws. Then, without much delay, their lives will be set in harmony with the entire nature, the whole universe. Maharishi emphasizes that the purity of the system has to be maintained generation after generation at any cost because, the effect of Transcendental Meditation depends upon the purity of the teaching. To maintain the purity of the system, the teachers of meditation should be trained thoroughly both in the practice and theory of Transcendental Meditation so that the system retains its purity and is passed on to the people in its pure state.

Maharishi emphasizes that to maintain the purity of the system it is necessary that teachers be found in all parts of the world, and that they have their own premises from which they work and impart teaching. It is necessary that centers of meditation which are the temples of human evolution are constructed every where in the world, so that, the teachers dedicated to the spreading of Transcendental Meditation continue to work and function from these centers, generation after generation with ease and facility.

7.   To maintain the teaching, generation after generation and for all times to come, Maharishi says it is necessary that the practice of this meditation, should somehow be made part and parcel of the daily routine of people. It should fall in the pattern of life of the people and should be a way of life. For this to happen it is necessary that sanctuaries of silence be constructed, in the midst of noisy market places of big cities. In such silent centers of meditation people before going to their business and after completing their business of the day may enter these silent chambers of meditation, dive deep within themselves, and be profited by undisturbed, regular and deep meditation. He also recommends that apart from these meditation centers in the noisy areas of the town, such meditation centers may also be constructed in the holiday resorts where people go on weekends and stay for one or two days. There, they may have the advantage of long hours of meditation and come home renewed in spirit, intelligence and energy.

He makes an appeal to the lovers of life, and well wishers of humanity, that they may start a programme of constructing these silent places of meditation to bring about spiritual regeneration by way of spreading the practical message of harmony and peace in life throughout the world.

Speaking about the importance of the organizations having their own premises, Maharishi gives the example that the history of different religions shows that it is the temples, churches, mosques and pagodas that have retained the voice of wisdom which characterize the supremacy of the various religions. He says that it is only such edifices that have contributed towards the retention of the voice of wisdom through the ages. But for these edifices the message of wisdom would have been lost long ago. The edifices stand as the living symbol of the message of wisdom. Although by themselves, they are not able to carry the message, their very presence will speak silently of the existence of a useful method to liberate mankind. It is as if, the buildings serve as the home of the ideology. Maharishi mentions of both body and spirit being needed to have an effective personality. Without the body the spirit will not be found and without the spirit the body will not function. So the spirit of the message will be the realized, or, evolved state of the teachers, and the purity of the system. The body of the message will be these buildings and the books, that will stand and help to preserve the spirit of the message.

Maharishi observes that the message if it has to be carried from generation to generation, should be placed on the mass psychology of each generation. It is found that the general understanding and tendencies of the people keep on changing from time to time. He points out, that there was a time when the religions had the upper hand and guided the destiny of the people. But when the message of the religions failed to provide a means to peace and inner harmony, and a direct way to God realization, then, people lost faith in religion. When religion is reduced to ritual and dogma only, the human mind, in its attempt to find a true understanding of life, turns to philosophy in its quest of truth on the intellectual basis. Dogmatic religions lose their importance and naturally go into the background of mass consciousness.

He points out that until recently about a hundred years ago the religions held sway over the people, over the mass consciousness. When the religions lost their hold on the mind of the society metaphysical movements combined with the comparative study of different religions became predominant. Thus the mass consciousness leaned on metaphysical studies. Even there, when metaphysics inspite of its endeavour to describe the reality failed to offer any practical formula for the realization of the abstract metaphysical truth, the human mind wanted to turn to something else.

The study of philosophy remained the interest of a few in the society. But the mass consciousness shifted towards the political awakening. The advent of the democratic ideology resulted in the mass consciousness being caught up in the vortex of democratic movements which participated in the day-to-day activities of political affairs in the respective countries. In a democracy each man is supposed to exercise his sovereignty and rule himself. As the democratic government became more and more predominant, political consciousness became the dominant factor in the life of the people. People began to look more and more to politics for the fulfillment of their lives. Politics had its sway over the life of the people, even though politics was not the platform to look to, for fulfillment of their life's aspirations. Politics is not a field to provide an adequate formula for the fulfillment of life of the individual. But, as of today, politics seems to have the upper hand over mass consciousness. Anything that happens in the field of politics receives attention and wide publicity. People talk about it and it attracts the attention of all nations. Then, as time went on economics began to influence the destiny of politics in many countries, and the advent of the socialist ideology and the cry for the structural adjustment of society and state on the basis of the social needs of the people galvanized the mass consciousness of the countries, under the leadership of Russia, China and the other socialist countries. These countries embarked on a plan of restructuring the state and society, on the basis of the socialist pattern. But, very recently these movements received a set back when the Russian socialist experiment and that of the East European countries collapsed. These countries were thrown into political and economic chaos, and the rise of a new order, is yet to dawn.

All this shows that the teaching of Transcendental Meditation cannot be placed on the basis of any rigid formula. It should be based on the basis of the changing consciousness of the masses and life of the people existing at the particular time. The policy of its propagation should accept the change in the level of mass consciousness at any time. It is only then that it could be easily imparted to all the peoples in every generation for the fulfillment of their life's aspirations.

When religion dominates the mass consciousness Transcendental Meditation should be taught in terms of religion. If metaphysical thinking rules the consciousness of society, Transcendental Meditation should be taught in metaphysical terms openly aiming at the fulfillment of the current metaphysical thought.

Whenever and wherever politics dominates the mass consciousness, Transcendental Meditation should recognize the political aspirations of the people and should be taught in terms of, and from the platform of politics, aiming at bringing fulfillment to the political aspirations of the generation. When economics dominates the mass consciousness, it should be taught to the goals and aspirations of the time.

Speaking about the present times, when politics is guiding the destiny of man, Maharishi points out, that the teaching should be primarily based on the field of politics and secondarily on the plane of economics. It will then be much easier to spread it in all countries and make it not only popular but practically available to all the peoples every where to serve the purpose of life.

Maharishi says that Transcendental Meditation should be made available to the people through the agencies of Government, because, any effort to propagate a new and useful ideology without the help of the government can ever succeed. It is the governments of the democratic countries that command the faith and goodwill of their people. The leaders of the government are the representatives of the peoples of the countries. Every leader naturally wishes to do something good for the people whom he represents. Therefore Transcendental Meditation which is a means for doing good to every individual, would certainly be accepted for its truth and value by all the leaders in different countries, and through them, it could be easily and effectively propagated throughout the world.

Maharishi recommends that on account of the great benefits of Transcendental Meditation in the fields of health, education, social welfare as well as for the lives of prisoners in jail and for the misguided lives of delinquents, it is highly useful if Transcendental Meditation is imparted to the people through the governmental agencies of health, education, social welfare and justice.

It should be a practice adopted by the medical profession, by teachers and professors in schools and colleges, by social workers who are concerned with improving the behaviour of the people within a society, and by all the well wishers of life in every field.

Maharishi emphasizes that the proper plan for the emancipation of all mankind, generation after generation, lies in training evolved teachers of Transcendental Meditation, constructing suitable silent sanctuaries for the meditation, bringing it to every individual on the basis of his need, his faith and his nature, and finding various ways and means for its propagation according to the mass consciousness of the people which holds sway at the time.

Maharishi concludes that the maintenance of the purity of the teaching will help the people of all times to mitigate their sufferings, overcome their short comings, and to remove their ignorance. It helps in ushering in a new era for a new humanity, developed in all the values of life, namely physical, mental, and spiritual. It doest enable man to live a life of fulfillment, established in eternal freedom in God consciousness.

The peace and prosperity of people everywhere will be secured in their evolved consciousness and status in higher values of life. This would result in man's accomplishment on the level of family, society, national and international planes to the maximum possible extent. Thus man will be destined naturally to live in fulfillment of all values from generation to generation.

1167122

Made in the USA